C000224629

Author's Note

In 1992 I was asked by East Hampshire District Council to write a playscript on the subject of the Selborne workhouse riot of 1830. Since I live in the neighbouring village of Headley, I was well aware that we'd also had a workhouse riot in the same year, and rumour said the people who did it came from Selborne. "Typical!", I thought. I knew very little more than that, but it seemed to me that it would be interesting, and still within the terms of East Hampshire's brief, to trace the connection between the two events in the play.

So began what seemed like a never-ending trail of fact-finding, matching and interpreting, as more and more interviews, visits, reading and re-reading produced ever more conflicting evidence and ambiguity. Eventually a story emerged which differed in some important and interesting aspects from that which local legends had previously suggested.

Then I had to shoe-horn the facts into a script, remembering that plays must also entertain as well as educate. Inevitably many compromises had to be made: invented dialogue was written to make the characters come alive on the stage, and many hard-gained pieces of information which would have lengthened the play without adding to its dramatic effect were excluded. The play is therefore not a strictly accurate record of the facts.

So in order to redress the balance, I decided to publish a more complete account of the collected information in book form, and **'One Monday in November'** *is the result. I don't profess to have dug as deeply for my facts as other researchers, since I started out looking only for enough information to write a play, not a learned treatise, and I have relied very heavily on the previous work of others, whose valuable assistance I hope I have acknowledged adequately.*

What I believe I may have done for the first time is to pull together the known information on two truly dramatic November days and their aftermath in a particular way, by following our band of local men as they marched along the lanes and tracks through this part of East Hampshire to do what they could to relieve their poverty. I hope you find it as fascinating to read as I did to write.

John Owen Smith
Headley, 1993

Foreword

Jo Smith's book is a real contribution to our history. It tells the story of a few tragic days in East Hampshire in 1830, when hungry men, bewildered by falling wages and rising prices, blundered into mob action. They wrecked two buildings, in a period when property was sacred - and retribution was savage - but strangely selective.

1830 - fifteen years since Waterloo and the defeat of revolutionary France, but years of depression and city riots! Now it was the turn of the countryside, where the hardships of the poor had been increased by low wages, enclosures and new machinery. In August the farm-workers of Kent suddenly broke out in riot and destruction. Mobs roamed the countryside carrying banners inscribed 'Bread or Blood', demanding money, firing ricks and destroying machines. Could England too be drifting towards revolution? The flame spread rapidly westwards. Our turn came in late November. The disturbances in Selborne and Headley were closely connected - in time, targets and cast of characters. In Liphook itself the mob was dispersed by firm action - but Liphook men almost certainly joined in the violence at Headley. In Jo Smith's book the events in the three villages are at last told as one coherent story.

I am particularly happy to have the chance to introduce the book to the public. A few years ago I researched and wrote a brief account of the riots, so I am probably one of the few people who can appreciate fully how hard Mr Smith must have worked, how thorough and widespread his investigations have been, unearthing ten times more information than I found. He gives us the economic and social background and then recounts the facts, with clarity, humour and impartiality. His sympathies are clear, but he has not made all his rich men villains or all his poor men saints; he has told it "as it happened". Selborne, Headley and Liphook are much in his debt.

L.C.Giles
Vice-Chairman, Bramshott and Liphook Preservation Society

One Monday
in November ...

The Story of the

Selborne and Headley

Workhouse Riots of 1830

To my parents, Doreen and Les,
whose fascination for history
I seem to have inherited.

View east across The Plestor, Selborne late C18th
(Vicarage out of picture behind wall on the left)

One Monday in November ...

... in the year 1830, a mob several hundred strong attacked the workhouse in Selborne, Hampshire, turned out the occupants, burned or broke the fittings and furniture, and pulled down the roof. The next day an even larger mob, containing some of the Selborne rioters, did the same to the workhouse at Headley, some 7 miles away. The parsons in both villages were also coerced into promising to reduce by half the income they took from tithes.

Less than a month later, at a special court hearing in Winchester attended by no less a person than the Duke of Wellington, nine local men were sentenced to transportation (commuted from a death sentence in the case of eight of them), and all but one sailed for the antipodes in the Spring of 1831 never to return.

These are the bare bones of the story. But why did the riot start? Why were the two workhouses attacked? And why were some of the supporters and leaders of the mobs seen to be not oppressed labourers, but relatively well-to-do artisans and farmers?

In this book we cover the dramatic events of the two days and their aftermath, piecing together the sometimes contradictory reports and legends which have grown up during intervening years around the names and deeds of those involved in the action.

Calendar of Events

November 1830

Sa 20 Selborne: Shots fired at the Harrisons
Mo 22 Selborne: Workhouse sacked, Cobbold mobbed
Liphook disturbance
Tu 23 Headley/Kingsley events
We 24 Wyck threshing machine damaged
Th 25 Budd reports 13 taken to Liphook

Dates of warrants: *Committed by:*

Fr 26	Thomas Robinson	Headley workhouse	*Budd*
	Robert Holdaway	Headley workhouse	*Budd*
	Thomas Marshall	Headley / Robbery	*Budd*
	William Bicknell	Headley workhouse	*Budd*
Mo 29	William Heighes	Wyck threshing machine	*RN Lee*
	Thomas Heighes	Wyck threshing machine	*RN Lee*
	John Newland	Mobbing vicar	*Knight/Hugonin*
Tu 30	John Heath	Headley workhouse	*Hugonin*

December 1830

Th 2	Henry James	Headley workhouse	*Budd*
	James Painter	Headley workhouse	*Budd*
	William Bright	Robbery in Headley	*Budd*
	Thomas Hoare	Selborne workhouse	*JBC*
Sa 4	Matthew Triggs	Headley workhouse	*JBC*
	Thomas Harding	Headley workhouse	*JBC*
	Henry Bone	Selborne workhouse	*JBC*
	Aaron Harding	Headley workhouse	*JBC*
	John Cobb	Selborne workhouse	*JBC*
Mo 6	John Trimming	Mobbing vicar	*Hugonin*
Tu 14	William Hoare	Selborne workhouse	*Hugonin*
We 15	Benjamin Smith	Selborne workhouse	*Hugonin*
	Robert Bennett	Selborne workhouse	*Hugonin*
	John Kingshott	Robbery in Kingsley	*Budd*

Mo 20 Special Commission started work in Winchester
Th 23 Trial: Selborne workhouse
Mo 27 Trial: Headley workhouse
We 29 Trial: Mobbing Selborne vicar
Th 30 Sentences passed: Holdaway 'left for execution'

January 1831

Sa 1 Cowburn wrote to Vaughan
Mo 3 Cowburn wrote to Lord Melbourne
Cobbold went to see Lord Melbourne
Th 6 Melbourne replied to Cowburn
Fr 7 Wellington wrote to Cowburn
Sa 8 Holdaway respited till 5th February
Tu 11 Thomas Heighes transferred to hulk *York*
We 12 James Bridger wrote to Cowburn
Sa 15 Execution of Cook and Cooper
Mo 31 Holdaway's counsel wrote to Melbourne

February 1831

Dates transferred to hulk York: *Sailed in:*

Th 3	Henry James		*Eleanor*
Sa 5	Matthew Triggs		*Eleanor*
	Aaron Harding		*Eleanor*
Su 6	Thomas Heighes sailed in *Eliza*;	arr. Tasmania 29 May	
Tu 8	John Heath		*Eleanor*
We 9	Robert Holdaway		*Eleanor*
	John Kingshott		*Proteus*
Th 10	Thomas Harding		*Proteus*
	James Painter		Not transported
Sa 19	*Eleanor* sailed	Arrived NSW on 25th June	

March 1831

Tu 1 James Painter   Transferred to hulk *Hardy*

April 1831

Th 14 *Proteus* sailed   Arrived Tasmania on 4th August

Note that the dates on the warrants are almost certainly later than the dates of actual arrest. In Liphook, where Henry Budd stated in a letter to John Bonham-Carter (JBC) on 25th November that he and John Coles had already 'taken' 13 men, the warrants for five of the men he named are not dated until over a week later.

Background

After Waterloo

Like 1066, the year 1815 is one which is well known to most scholars, and generally assumed to be a 'good thing' - the final victory over Napoleon by the allies at Waterloo. But this victory, and the ensuing peace in Europe, was the beginning of the end as far as the English agricultural labourer was concerned.

There had already been a steady move by law-makers and large land-owners in the country away from supporting the traditional land-owning peasant, able to grow some of his own food and keep a few animals, towards using the wage-earning labourer who had no land of his own and relied entirely on the money he earned to subsist. During the Napoleonic wars, labour was scarce and wages therefore relatively high, but after Waterloo, returning soldiers swelled the available workforce, and labour was no longer at a premium.

Problems of falling wages and rising prices inevitably led to discontent, and in some cases abject poverty among the labourers and their dependants, and so-called 'bread or blood' riots broke out in East Anglia and elsewhere. By the time the autumn of 1830 came round, some particularly bad harvests in the previous two summers and a severe winter in between had set the scene for another period of agitation. But now there were other influences which made the uprisings more significant than before.

Across the Channel, revolutions were still occurring in France, and also in Belgium which gained its independence from Holland in November of that year. In Britain, King George IV died during the summer, his brother William succeeded to the throne, and a general election changed the government from Tory to Whig for the first time in many years. So a new, untried administration was looking nervously across the water at a Europe once again in turmoil, and seeing any signs of local revolt in this country as a possible start to a larger and more serious civil conflict.

But such unrest had been predicted earlier in the year, when William Cobbett reflected that he would "better be a dog than a farmer next winter." And when the traditional 'doling' period of the year arrived, that time between the end of harvest and the start of the new year when the labourer's work is at its minimum and consequently he has more time in which to reflect on his lack of earnings, the customary gatherings and perambulations of labourers to exact money and food from the better-off villagers turned into something altogether more serious.

Starting in Kent during the early autumn these disturbances, which have become known as the 'Swing Riots', swept across southern England and reached Hampshire in the second week of November. Nobody quite knows how the movement spread, but at the time the government convinced itself that it was the work of French spies, or travelling Methodist ministers, or a plot co-ordinated by a self-styled 'Captain Swing', whose name was at the bottom of some of the posters and threatening letters which began to appear. They could not believe simply that the circumstances of the village labourer, and to a degree the village tradesmen and small farmers, had become so unbearable that word of a riot succeeding and forcing an increase in wages and a reduction of rates in one village would be enough to spark a 'copy cat' rising in the next.

The actions taken by rioters differed from place to place, depending on local circumstances and local grievances. In many locations threshing machines, first introduced in the 1780s but now becoming more widespread, were seen to be taking away the winter livelihood of the labourer and became a target. In other places parsons were mobbed and forced to sign agreements to take less in tithes from the land, or magistrates urged to declare a general raise in wages in their area. Selborne and Headley were almost unique in that, along with the more common actions, the mobs also ransacked the workhouses (poor houses) there.

Selborne in 1830

Selborne was not a happy place during this period. William Cobbett, when staying there overnight on one of his 'Rural Rides' in 1823, reported that he met a local man who told him that "he did not believe there was a more unhappy place in England" than Selborne. When asked why, he replied that "there's always quarrels of some sort or other going on ... on matters of rates and tithes mostly." Cobbett then remembered he had read about a shot being fired through the vicar's window, and a King's proclamation for a reward relating to the discovery of the perpetrator. Nobody came forward to claim the reward.

The vicar in question, William Rust Cobbold, was not well loved in his parish. He was regarded as arrogant by his parishioners, and on his own admission seemed to be in constant conflict with his vestry. For a parish which could still remember the gentle curacy of Gilbert White, this must have been an unhappy situation indeed. We have records of acrimonious notes passing between him and the officials of the parish, and of court actions taken by him and them. Following the events of 1830 he acquired a mastiff dog with a neck 'as thick as a lion's' for his protection; its collar can be seen to this day in the church.

The vestry would meet in the public house, where they "knew the vicar would not go", he claiming to be the "only gentleman in the village". It is therefore perhaps not surprising to find that the ex-landlord of this pub, who had been expelled from this position by Cobbold and who some sources say was a member of the Selborne vestry, played a leading role in the events which unfolded in the village and spilt over into neighbouring parishes.

Headley in 1830

By contrast the rector at Headley, described as a "jolly, big old Cumbrian farmer who suffered from ill-health and was a good deal absent from the village", seems to have been regarded in a more kindly light by his flock. He was present in the village at the time of the riot, and the difference between his attitude and that of the vicar of Selborne can be seen by the fact that he <u>was</u> prepared to attend a meeting in the village pub to discuss labourers wages.

Although as a bald statement of fact similar events happened in Headley as in Selborne, the parson was 'mobbed' to reduce his tithes and the workhouse was sacked, the actions here seem to have been directed less at personalities and more at the institutions they represented.

That is not to say there were no differences of opinion in Headley - what village could exist without them? There was, for example, a public poster-debate in 1822 between certain small farmers of the parish and the Guardians of the Poor as to what should be regarded as 'fair and reasonable' labourers' wages. The small farmers thought six shillings a week for a labourer over 20 years of age was adequate, while the Guardians thought eight or nine shillings more reasonable. In 1830 the cry was for twelve shillings, but we have records from 1843 showing that nine shillings continued to be the going rate in Headley.

Parish of Headley.

To Mr. THOMAS MARNER WALKER, and FRANCIS BRYANT, Guardians of the Poor of the Parish of Headley, in the County of Southampton, and to each of them.

WE, the undersigned, Daniel Knight, (Collecting Overseer,) Robert Parker, John Clear, William Swann, Edward Keen, George Baker, John Fisher, and Richard Knight, Junr. Occupiers of Messuages, Lands, Tenements, and Hereditaments, rated and rateable to the Poor, in the said Parish of Headley, Do hereby give you and each of you Notice, that We are willing and desirous of employing Paupers in the Parish, at the Wages of Six Shillings per Week each, being fair and reasonable Wages at this Time, when the Price of Corn is very low, and the Bread is consequently cheap; and that the receipt of Money for Agricultural Produce by Farmers is so much reduced, that no one can pay more for common Labour than at the rate of Six Shillings per Week; and for as much as you, or one of you, as Guardians of the Poor of Headley, have lately been in the habit of employing many of the Labourers on the Highways, and otherwise, at Wages of Eight Shillings a Week, from the Money collected on the Poor Rates, We consider ourselves aggrieved, because the Poor Rates are thereby greatly increased, to the grievous Injury of ourselves and all those who pay Poor Rates in the Parish!

Part of a Poster issued by small farmers of Headley in May 1822

Village Finances

Since the whole argument of the riots was over money, it is important to understand the social and financial structure of a village at that time.

At the top of the tree there was normally a large landowner, possibly a Lord of the Manor, to whom the majority of the villagers and the parson would owe allegiance. But in Selborne and Headley this was not the case; neither village had a resident Lord of the Manor nor a significant single landowner at that time. Hobsbawm and Rudé in their book *Captain Swing* tend to see the lack of such a restraining influence as being one of the factors making a village susceptible to riot.

The Tithes

The parson in a village lived on the tithes which were due to him from the parish, plus the proceeds of any other activity he might pursue or land he might possess. Tithes were originally introduced as long ago as 750 AD, being payable in kind as a tenth (= *tithe)* of the produce of the land to the 'tithe-holder'. In the case of a Rector, he was due both the 'great' or rectorial tithes (corn, beans, peas, hay and wood) and the 'small' or vicarial tithes (the remainder); a Vicar was only due the small tithes, the great tithes going to some other holder - in the case of Selborne, to Magdalen College, Oxford.

The massive tithe barns which still exist around the country were built to store the corn, hay, wood and other commodities due to the church each year. But it was always a problem for the parson or tithe-holder physically to collect such tithes, particularly if landowners were reluctant to deliver and he had to arrange himself for the produce to be brought in. Roads in those days, it must be remembered, were still dirt tracks and often ankle deep or worse in mud. So by 1830 it had become common practice for the Church to collect tithes in money, at an agreed exchange rate equivalent to the value of the produce that would otherwise be due, or for them to sell the rights to 'farm the tithes' to the highest bidder.

But this sum tended to become fixed over a period of time, and not reflect the natural fluctuations of good and lean years.

Thus after two poor harvests in 1829 and 1830, farmers found they still had to hand over the same amount of money to the tithe-holder as in a good year, even though they had less produce to sell in order to pay for it.

The Poor Rate

Moreover, tithes were not the only taxes due from landowners. There were also land taxes to be paid, and in addition each parish was charged with looking after its own Poor, and the funds for this were levied by applying a local Poor Rate, which was paid according to the rateable value of property. The rate was agreed periodically by officers of the parish according to their need for funds, and the definition as to who was and was not a pauper, and therefore able to claim 'on the parish', was a point of continual argument. Real poverty, to the extent of actual starvation, was far from unknown in the rural communities of the time, and in 1795 a group of Berkshire magistrates concerned to raise labourers' wages to a subsistence level met at the Pelican Inn, Speenhamland (now part of Newbury), and made what turned out to be a momentous decision, gradually adopted across most of England.

Instead of raising wages, or more precisely fixing them to the current price of bread as had been intended, the meeting chose to supplement existing low wages from the parish fund (the Poor Rate) up to the intended figure. This decision produced almost the opposite effect to that desired. It meant that labourers could now receive a minimum wage for doing nothing, although generally the parish found work for the able-bodied to do, such as repairing roads, or hiring them out to farmers at an agreed rate. It also meant that farmers were not encouraged to pay 'reasonable' wages, since they knew the Poor Rate would pay the shortfall. *(See the Appendix on Labour Rates in 1830 for more details).* Granted the farmers were also among those contributing to the Poor Rate by way of taxes, but this load was shared between all the other property-owning parishioners who then begrudged the fact that they were subsidising the farmers' labour. The farmers pointed to the high tithes as an excuse for not being able to pay more.

A Report of the Poor Law Commissioners in 1835 said, *'Many farmers dismiss workers even from profitable employment to make others assist in maintaining them. They do not want to see their neighbours have a lighter burden in helping the poor.'* And in the middle of this argument, the labourers and their families saw no escape from the poverty trap. The Settlement Acts made it difficult for them to move to find better jobs (other parishes would only allow them to stay if their 'home parish' certified that they would take them back if they could not support themselves), and if they resorted to poaching, which was the only other real means of improving their lot, the penalty was transportation or death - or a maiming for life in a man-trap, which was almost as bad.

The Poor Houses

For those who had no other home, the parish provided accommodation in Poor Houses, or workhouses as they were more commonly referred to. While these were never places of ease, the original concept of having a number of small houses in which families could be kept together was at least tolerable. However, in an attempt to encourage those who could get out and work to do so, a policy began to be adopted in which paupers were brought together to live in larger 'Union' buildings which were purposely made to be cheerless and uncomfortable. In these, families would be segregated by sex and a tough regime adopted. Residents could not go out or see visitors without the permission of the Master, who was often running the workhouse on a franchise basis to make a living for himself and his family.

While a more general move to create 'Union' Houses occurred later as a result of the 1834 Poor Law, the idea had started as early as the 1770s, and Selborne and Headley (along with Alton) appear to have been forward in their thinking. The Selborne building was purchased in 1794 for £250 from James Knight, and the Headley 'House of Industry' was built in 1795 at an estimated cost of some £1,500 for the parishes of Headley, Bramshott and Kingsley, to shelter their infirm, aged paupers, and orphan or illegitimate children. To add to their degradation, all who received parish relief in Headley wore a badge on their clothing to proclaim the fact, with the metal letters 'HP' for Headley Poor.

Why the Riot?

If the tithes could be reduced, then the farmers could, in theory at least, pay the difference in higher wages to their labourers, and perhaps even take on more labour than before. This would stop the need for payment of 'parish relief' to these labourers and their families, which would then reduce the Poor Rate payments of all tax payers in the parish. In short, everyone would seem to gain from it except the clergy, and possibly the master of the Poor House who would be given less money to dispense. The main target of the villagers was therefore the Church tithes, which were seen as an unnecessary drain on parish resources, and in Selborne, at least, as going into the pocket of an unpopular man.

But the church would not give up its traditional income willingly. The only way that hard-pressed parishioners could see of achieving their aim was by using force of numbers, and as a result many vicars and rectors in the south of England were 'mobbed' during the 1830 disturbances, usually with labourers to the fore and farmers and other tax-paying tradesman urging them on from behind. In this way the labourers took the brunt of the retribution handed out in subsequent trials, even though their masters and social betters were likely to gain as much if not more than they from any reductions obtained. Of the 22 men known to have been arrested following the Selborne and Headley riots, all but three or four were agricultural labourers; Holdaway, Heath, Triggs and possibly James were the exceptions, and not one farmer was arrested.

So we can see a logical argument as to why the parishioners of a village should want to 'mob' their parson - but it is more difficult to understand why they attacked the Poor Houses. In this, Selborne and Headley were, as previously noted, almost unique. Hobsbawm & Rudé in *Captain Swing* record other instances of Overseers being attacked, but not of other Poor Houses being sacked. Certainly there would seem to have been no real benefit for the farmers, the tradesmen, or the rioters to have the Poor Houses destroyed. The short answer is, we don't know why; but it may be that other 'rioting' villages did not have such obvious, invidious and undefended targets to attack. It seems that while the crowd's blood was up in Selborne and Headley, they felt they might as well use it as an excuse to 'have a go' at the hated Union *Werk'uses*. But while this may go some way to explaining the Selborne incident, the Headley sacking appears to have been far more premeditated, and therefore less explicable in this way.

Premeditated or not, it certainly seems as though the activities of the mob got out of hand on the day. It is not clear what control either the farmers or Robert Holdaway and the other tradesmen expected to exercise over events, but as the judge said when summing up Holdaway's case, "I hope that the events of this day will mark an awful lesson to any who may hereafter think of engaging in such deeds of outrage; I hope that they will teach such persons it may be impossible to check or control the disorderly spirits whom they may have called into action to effect their own wicked and illegal purposes." We may dispute whether they were wicked, or even whether everything they were accused of was strictly illegal, but there is no doubt that where a mob of people is involved, the heart often rules the head and little account is taken by those involved at the time of what may seem sensible in retrospect.

Robert Holdaway's signature
in Selborne vestry minutes of 11th April 1823

Selborne, Saturday 20th - Monday 22nd November, 1830

The Saturday Dole

On the Saturday before the disturbances, the labourers and paupers of Selborne were doled out their weekly allowance from the parish as normal. It seems that they received this from Mr John Harrison, referred to in contemporary *Times* reports as the 'guardian', who was the Master of the Poor House there.

We are not sure whether the recipients went down to the Poor House to receive their dole, or whether it was given out to them at some other location in the village, but on this particular occasion Mr Harrison recollected that some of them "expressed their intention of going round to the farmers to make them raise their wages." He said he "advised them not to do so, or they would repent hereafter." It could have been normal banter, but later events showed that on this day the complaints held a greater significance.

However, it was not the farmers who they went round to next, but Mr Harrison himself. He was obviously not a popular man. He was referred to by Holdaway's counsel as being "particularly obnoxious to the poor of the neighbourhood", and another correspondent recalled an incident "which exited a universal feeling of disgust" when it was discovered that some of the inmates were chained to the wall. The *Times* records that "about 12 o'clock in the night of the same day three guns, loaded with slugs, were discharged into the bed-room of Mr Harrison at the workhouse, and although the clothes and furniture of the bed were completely torn to pieces by the slugs, we are happy to say none of the family were wounded."

Sunday, 21st November

It is doubtful whether the next day was a Day of Rest for many in the village, and it would be interesting to know what sermon the Reverend William Cobbold chose to read out in St Mary's church that morning. We can imagine the impromptu meetings which must have gone on as the parishioners left the south door after matins and ducked under the boughs of the old yew tree: farmers consulting each other, and walking

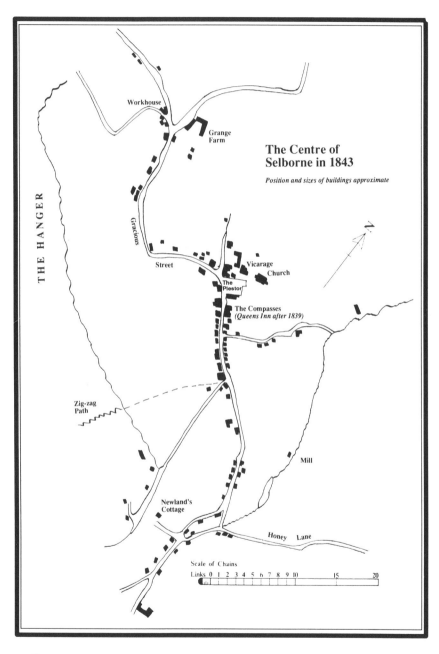

The Centre of Selborne in 1843

Position and sizes of buildings approximate

THE HANGER

Workhouse

Grange Farm

Gracious

Street

Vicarage

Church

The Plestor

The Compasses
(Queens Inn after 1839)

Zig-zag Path

Mill

Newland's Cottage

Honey Lane

Scale of Chains

Links 0 1 2 3 4 5 6 7 8 9 10   15   20

together up the main street to *The Compasses* to finish the discussion over a beer; tradesmen and artisans likewise involved; and groups of labourers perhaps organising their own meetings away from the eye of their masters. But this is conjecture.

We are told by James Bridger, a farmer of Oakhanger, in a letter written later at the request of William Cowburn, a London solicitor whose family lived part of the year in the village, that the farmers first heard on Sunday morning that there was to be a mob at Selborne. Hori Hale (another farmer) and Henry Collyer (a churchwarden) went to Cobbold to ask his advice, but "he was very short with them and told them they might do as they thought fit; for his part he could do nothing".

Mrs Cowburn reported that men climbed into the yew tree overlooking the vicarage on Sunday evening to make sure Cobbold would not get away in the night.

Monday Morning, Outside the Vicarage

The next thing we are told is that at seven o'clock on Monday morning Cobbold, as he left the vicarage, observed two or three of his own labourers among a group of 7 or 8 talking together. He then saw Aaron Harding join the men, and when he asked them what they were going to do Harding told him they were going to "turn out old Harrison", and that they must have their wages raised to 12 shillings a week.

Aaron Harding was a 41 year old labourer, widowed the previous year and with nine children aged between two and twenty. He was later described by the vicar as being "desperate and daring". We know from the Poor Book records that three years earlier he was receiving a dole from the parish of 12 shillings a week, made up of seven shillings for his 6 youngest children, 2/6d for his wife and 2/6d for himself, but we do not know what he was receiving at the time of the riot.

The vicar told him that he saw no objection to wages of 12 shillings a week, as he paid at least that sum to his own labourers, and "to some 14 shillings besides giving them in addition a cottage and a garden." Given his general unpopularity within the village, it seems unlikely that this would endear him further to the other employers of labour who had to fund their wage bill from the land, while the Cobbold received a substantial sum in tithes from which to pay his expenses.

Bridger's letter says that the farmers had called a meeting a few days before and agreed to "advance the labourers' wages to 2/- a day", in order to prevent the sort of riots in Selborne that were happening elsewhere; however Cowburn himself declares that "the farmers deliberated, but came to no decision."

We deduce that a discussion of some sort between the farmers and labourers of Selborne must have occurred however, for Harding then said to the vicar, "We must have a touch of your tithes." Cobbold first of all seemed to treat this as a joke. stating that if his income was reduced he "could not do the good he was in the habit of doing", and pointing out to Harding that he had been particularly kind to his family, which we assume referred to the time of his bereavement the previous year. Harding was in no mood for compromise however, and said the tithes must be reduced to £300 a year, adding that this was "quite enough and according to our regulation." It is not clear whose regulation he meant, but by implication it probably came from the farmers. John Trimming (25), another of the rioters whose name we know from later committal proceedings, is reported to have added that £4 a week was quite enough for Cobbold, leaving us to wonder which was wrong, his arithmetic or our information.

The vicar must have asked who was going to persuade him to do this, for Harding then told him they had "a large party" and asked him to come and look at them. A contemporary report mentions that "a mob about 300 in number, collected from the surrounding country, had entered Selborne armed with large clubs, etc." Cobbold presumably declined the invitation to view them, and said he would not submit to a reduction in tithes, whereupon Harding remarked that "the farmers have undertaken to raise our wages, and we have undertaken to reduce the tithes."

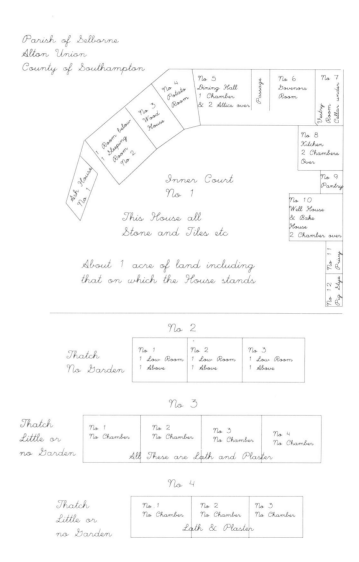

Plan of Selborne Workhouse
prepared February 1836 in preparation for its sale

We assume that the interview ended at this point, for we next hear that at nine o'clock the vicar "saw two flags and a mob of three or four hundred." As well as Aaron Harding he also mentions by name John Cobb who, he says, "was very drunk and took a very violent part", and Robert Holdaway of whom we will hear much more later. They repeated to him their object of raising wages and reducing tithes, then Harding said, "We shall go now and turn out old Harrison first, and then come back to you; stop till we come back, or it will be the worse for you". Part of the mob went off down Gracious Street towards the workhouse "blowing a horn", and about fifty to one hundred others remained near his house, "so that they could watch my motions", as Cobbold later testified.

At the Poor House in Gracious Street

When the mob arrived at the Poor House they found that Mr Harrison was not at home, though his wife and family were. Considering the fact that he must have been aware something was going on, indeed Bridger claims that the farmers had warned him the evening before, we may find this strange; perhaps he had gone to seek help, perhaps away on unavoidable business - we do not know. The mob "gave the mistress of the house notice to quit before night", but she seems not unnaturally to have taken fright and left the house with her family almost immediately, some say through a back window.

Edward Ticknell recollected later in court how, on hearing that there was trouble, he had gone to the workhouse and found the mob there "pulling tiles off the roof, breaking up furniture and smashing windows." A fire had been started and he saw Bennett throwing water on it. "Newland was there, blowing his horn and carrying the flags", he said, and in less than 15 minutes the house was unroofed, the doors, crockery and windows broken, feather beds pulled to pieces, the furniture destroyed and burnt, and Harrison's grandfather clock thrown on the fire.

Mrs Cowburn mentions fires being started in several places, and that "young Debenham, having attempted to put them out, was almost demolished by the mob." Holdaway also, as

related by his counsel later, was "actively engaged in putting out the fire which threatened the destruction of the building."

However, the judge at the subsequent trial observed that "if the destruction of the workhouse had been intended, the fire would probably have been lit in the middle of the room, and not in the chimney as was the case", and guided the jury to declare that "the mob had only intended the destruction of part of the property, and not the whole." They therefore found all the accused 'not guilty', but the same prisoners were remanded to be indicted later for mobbing the vicar.

Later in the day, Bridger reports that Mr Debenham Snr arrived at Selborne and remonstrated with the mob on its being an "unlawful proceeding", but they immediately surrounded him with uplifted clubs and demanded to know what he meant. This, "with the treatment his son had received at the workhouse before", was enough to convince him that persuasion and not force would be the best option, as they were only a few unarmed men against 300.

The Same Day, at Liphook and Steep

Apparently Mrs Harrison fled with her family to Liphook, for we see in a letter written by Henry Budd JP to John Bonham-Carter the next day: "Yesterday they burnt the Poor House at Selborne with all poor Harrison's furniture and wearing apparel, and threatened to murder his family, which Mrs Dowling at the *Anchor* at Liphook has informed me are in her house, and it is said that the people mean to come over tomorrow and have them or destroy the house." He goes on to say that he had stationed soldiers there for their protection, and asks for reinforcements as speedily as possible. More evidence, if any were necessary, of the depth of hatred the people of Selborne felt towards their *Werk'us*, its Master and his family.

On the same day that Selborne was rioting, Liphook saw a disturbance of its own, at about two o'clock in the afternoon, when a "large and tumultuous assemblage" of 200 to 300 labourers met outside the *Anchor* to complain of low wages. The local men were apparently being incited by a person who was a stranger to the area. Mr Budd and other local landowners were there, trying to persuade them to disperse, when the Regulator coach arrived from London with Dr Quarrier, a magistrate from Steep, inside. He apparently sized up the situation, grabbed the stranger by the collar and, with the help of two constables, bundled him into the coach and sped off with him towards Petersfield, where he was committed and sent on to the Gosport Bridewell. We are told that the Liphook mob then dispersed with no further trouble.

The Anchor, Liphook in the mid 1800s

This same Dr Quarrier arrived home at Steep in the evening to consult with John Coles, another of the county's magistrates, and John Bonham-Carter, who was High Sheriff of Hampshire and also MP for Portsmouth, about a meeting of labourers organised by a self-styled 'General Committee' to take place the next day in Steep churchyard. They agreed to send round a request to all the farmers asking them not to allow their labourers to attend the meeting, and this measure succeeded in preventing both the Steep meeting and a subsequent one planned for Wednesday, which was market day, in Petersfield.

But no such remedial action occurred in Selborne or Headley.

Back Outside the Selborne Vicarage

Cobbold had been "expostulating for three quarters of an hour" with that part of the mob left outside his house when he "heard something and went towards the workhouse, and met some persons running in great fear" who warned him to "take care of himself, as the mob were coming back and bent on mischief."

Here we may imagine the somewhat amusing spectacle of the snobbish Rev Cobbold running quickly back to his house, where he waited until the mob returned to The Plestor. He again names Cobb, Trimming and Harding as those pressing against his gate, and he asked them what their object was. Cobb, who was probably still not sober, told him he must lower his tithes to £300 a year, and Harding "repeated the same in a very violent manner." Cobbold says he told them "they could not be in earnest." According to Cowburn, the mob, now swollen in number to over 400, gave Cobbold half an hour to make a decision, and "when that time had expired, just 5 minutes more", before "a rush was about to take place upon him and his house."

Apparently Holdaway was prominent in holding back the mob, and particularly Cobb, at this juncture. Bridger claims it was the farmers who asked him to do it, but Holdaway had his own reasons for being there. Cobbold had persevered for years to have Holdaway expelled from *The Compasses*, the only Public House in Selborne at the time, where he had been landlord. Cowburn writes: "I will not say Holdaway did not keep an irregular house, but I will say that, in my opinion, it was not worse than at neighbouring places." Cobbold had eventually succeeded in having him expelled, and Holdaway had been unemployed since. During the arguments that arose during the expulsion, it seems that Cobbold told Holdaway he would show him "no mercy." Holdaway was now able to turn the tables and embarrass the clergyman with a display of Christian charity, saying to him: "Now, sir, you once told me you would have no mercy on me - you see I have had mercy on you."

And here for the first time we see the direct involvement, or rather non-involvement, of the farmers. Cobbold says that several farmers (some reports say ten) were present, but they "merely looked on tamely." He claimed that one of them, who was High Constable, said it was no use to resist such a mob, and another, Hori Hale, said, 'For God's sake accept of £300 a year; if you don't you'll be murdered and your house pulled down.' Seeing such lack of support by those from whom he might reasonably have expected more, he "found it necessary to submit", adding that nothing but a firm conviction that he "should otherwise be destroyed" induced him to do so.

Mr Hale communicated to the mob that the vicar had agreed, at which they cheered and asked "to have it in black and white." Cobbold then sent Henry Eade, a churchwarden, into the house to draw up an agreement, and when it was brought out he signed it. The mob called for the farmers to witness it, which they did with a show of reluctance in some cases, and, when the contents of the paper had been read out, asked for a copy of it which Henry Eade duly went back into the house to make. The original was given by Mr H Cole, the vicar's bailiff, to farmer Bridger, and the copy given to a representative of the mob.

The mob then called for £5 for beer, which Cobbold says he "told them they should not have." He claims the farmers let him down again, for he says that "one of the principal farmers proposed that I should let them have £2 worth of beer, and put it down in the poor-book. I said, 'Do as you like.'" But Bridger's version of events is rather different, as he says that Cobbold "was the first to propose its being charged to the Parish account, and mentioned how much he thought each man should have." He also says that Henry Eade "wished half the beer to be had from his house", though he does not mention which house this might be. The farmers, he says, had "refused for some time to give any beer, and only consented at last on condition they (the mob) should immediately disperse and go to their work."

Whoever suggested it, the beer was ordered by the farmers from a public house, presumably *The Compasses*, and brought out in buckets to the men; and the bill which came to £3 17s was duly charged to the Poor Rate. Then the mob dispersed, having remained outside the vicarage and "conducted

themselves in a particularly violent manner" for three hours according to Cobbold. The farmers, strongly admonished later by the trial judge for their inaction, pleaded that they were forced to attend. We may rather think that they were there to ensure they got what they wanted out of the day's proceedings.

Cowburn says that the remainder of that night was passed by the mob in "eating, drinking and rioting." His wife wrote letters to him (for he was not himself in Selborne on this day) in which she says that the mob had stopped the Gosport Coach and one other carriage during the day and made them give money, but that she and her family were not troubled, even though they were "almost the only assailable family" in Selborne. Cowburn himself puts this down to his efforts, over the 8 or 9 years he had been living there, in being "attentive" to the poor of the parish, and giving "any poor man who desired it an acre or two each, to enable them to grow their own potatoes and wheat for bread." He records that when his manservant asked the mob collected at his gate what they wanted, they replied: "Nothing here; this gentleman and lady bear too good characters and are too good to the poor, and we will not hurt a stick or stone about them."

Holdaway and Newland

Two names which, for most people, are synonymous with the Selborne riot are those of Robert Holdaway and John Newland, the Ringleader and the 'Trumpeter' respectively. We have mentioned Holdaway's name already, but Newland's not at all, and it seems that both of their roles at Selborne may have been less than the popular legends would have us believe.

Robert Holdaway (37) is described as a carpenter, wheelwright, hop planter and former landlord of *The Compasses* (renamed the *Queens Inn* in 1839). Although sometimes referred to as a widower, he was at the time of the riot married to his second wife Sarah Freeman, daughter of a big butcher in Alresford, by whom he had five children then aged between one and eight. He also had two children aged 17 and 14 by a previous marriage to Elizabeth Mayhew. According to his children's baptism records, he appears to have moved to Selborne from the Alresford area in 1822/23, but we shall see later that he was also known in Headley and it seems likely that he was a relatively well travelled man around the locality. He was, as stated by Cowburn, currently unemployed due to his previous altercations with Cobbold.

Records of the time say that he was "chosen by the mob to take the agreement round to the neighbouring farmers to get them to sign it as well. This he agreed to do." The choice of Holdaway was approved by the farmers present, and his counsel later made the point that this was perhaps "because he was a man of more discretion than the rest." Apparently the signatures of several individuals in the Newton Valence and Hartley Mauditt areas were obtained later that same day, and Holdaway had proposed to proceed alone with the agreement to other places the next day, but "the mob would not hear of this and insisted they would accompany him." It would appear that he was at best a reluctant hero. At his trial, Harriet Freeman (his sister-in-law?) stated that she was at his house when the mob called on the Monday and forced him away, and he himself also stated at his trial that all he did was to "go about with the mob to prevent them from doing any mischief."

As a footnote, it is interesting to note vicar Cobbold's subsequent statements about Holdaway. At the trial, he said he had known Holdaway for 8 years, that he was of Selborne parish, and he would "rather not be asked" as to his character; but he also "begged to state, as an act of justice to Holdaway, that he saved his (Cobbold's) life and property on the 22nd by his influence over the mob that were about his house". Later, in March 1832, when a petition seems to have been raised on Holdaway's behalf for his return, Cobbold wrote of him as being "of notorious memory on account of the leading part he took in the riots of this neighbourhood." He obviously did not want to see him back in Selborne.

John Newland (39) was, "like all the Newlands", according to a grand-daughter of his, "a big strong man." He had seen service in the North Hampshire Regiment, and had collected a wound in the head while on service abroad which meant that even a small amount of drink affected him. He lived in a cottage in Adams Lane with his wife Ann and, in 1830, eight children (two by Ann's previous marriage) ranging in age from 12 years to six months. Records show the family receiving 11/6d a week from the Poor Rate in October 1827, made up of 8/- for his wife and his children, 2/6d for his wife's children and 1/- for an 'ill child'. He is described as a farm labourer, and at his trial was given a good character reference both by farmer Edward Fitt and by Cobbold himself, who said he was a quiet, inoffensive man, except when he had been drinking.

Legend says that he led the Selborne rioters and rallied them with his horn, but in his testimony at the trial he claims that he was pressed by Aaron Harding to leave his work on the Monday and go with them, that he blew his horn only once at the desire of some of the men, and that in the evening he was "knocked down by some of the party for not having taken an active part at the workhouse." He also implies that he followed the mob to Headley on the following day, but we hear no mention of him there. A warrant for his arrest was issued the following Monday for his part in the Selborne events.

There is a further popular legend that he escaped arrest by hiding in the woods above the village, coming down to his cottage at night for food. He may have evaded capture for a while by this means, but it would be for two nights at the most, since his testimony states that he "went to work and was taken on the Friday" following the riot, which would make him one of the earlier men to be picked up. It is interesting to note that one of the names on his warrant is E. Knight Jnr - could it be that, along with his other claims to fame, Newland was also arrested by Jane Austen's nephew?

Others arrested for the Selborne riot were: John Trimming (25), John Cobb (27), Benjamin Smith (23), William Bicknell (23), Thomas Hoare (36), William Hoare (39), Henry Bone (31), and Robert Bennett (16) - all labourers we think. Aaron Harding and Robert Holdaway were charged instead with events at Headley, which were regarded as more serious offences.

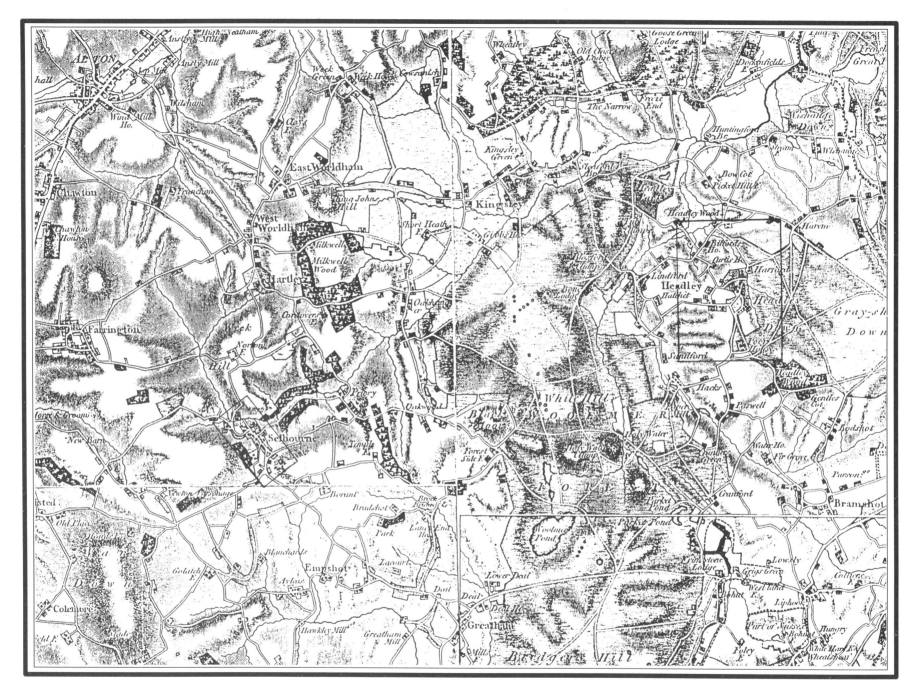

Alton - Liphook area: from 1" Ordnance Survey maps dated prior to 1815

To Headley and Kingsley, Tuesday 23rd November 1830

Why Headley?

We must now ask ourselves why the Selborne mob should, after they had seemingly achieved their own parochial ends, march some seven miles on a cold November day to Headley, in a neighbouring parish, to repeat the same procedure there.

Given that the population of adult males (over 20 years old) in Selborne was just under 200 at the time, some of the estimated 300 or more rioters present on the Monday must have come from outside the parish, as indeed contemporary reports imply. It may be that these included 'helpers' from Headley who came on a mutual understanding that assistance would be returned in kind on the following day - but this is pure conjecture on our part. Certainly John Heath, a master carpenter of Selborne parish with a house and shop, but a "desperate and daring" man according to Cobbold, had originally come from Headley and was very active in the subsequent destruction there.

Mrs Cowburn also tells her husband on Monday evening that the Selborne men were going tomorrow "to demolish the workhouse at Headleigh (*sic*) where young Harrison is." She does not make it clear whether she is referring to the master of Selborne workhouse or a son of his, or in what capacity he was there, and Headley records do not mention him, but it leaves the possibility that the move to Headley was in part at least a continuation of the Selborne vendetta against the Harrisons.

What we do know is that people in Headley were aware in advance that trouble was heading their way. At 8 o'clock on Tuesday morning Matthew Triggs and his brother William went to Headley Poor House to try to fetch out their uncle, a pauper named Tuckey, and take him down to their sisters, because they said they thought "there would be a row or a piece of work at the house that day". Mr James Shoesmith, the Master of Headley Poor House, refused to let him go saying, "No, I can't spare him, for if there is to be a row he can speak more and better to the purpose than any person else." He gave the Triggs brothers a pint of beer each and they went away - but Matthew was to return later.

In the meantime, the Selborne mob had "called on Robert Holdaway again this morning and pressed him to go with them to gather more signatures on their agreement." Apparently there were rumours that there was to be another attack made on Cobbold, but "this proved untrue and only about 60 Selborne and Oakhanger men came here this morning", according to Mrs Cowburn in Selborne. Her husband reports that on that morning "the banner was again displayed, their force called together by the sound of horns and, compelling all labourers everywhere to join, they accumulated it is said 1,100 and proceeded to Headley."

In fact there is reason to believe that this figure relates to their number by the time they had arrived at Headley, and that considerably fewer started from Selborne; but whatever the number, Selborne was very empty that day. The leaders of the mob appear to have pressed all the men in the village to their cause, with "threats used to those who deserted." Mrs Cowburn, in a letter written the following day, says "there was scarcely a man in the place", and describes how "the silence throughout the village, with here and there a woman or a child straggling about, was quite awful, and all sorts of reports were in circulation as to what was going on." She also said that the children would never forget 'the mob' - "they thought it fun at first, but then got rather frightened."

The mob went first to farms in the Empshott and Greatham area, and Cowburn says that at Empshott, Holdaway "stayed the fury of the worst man in the parish when directed against the chief farmer." From Greatham they set out for Headley where a meeting had been called by the farmers and the clergy there to discuss the issue of labourers wages. It was to take place at the *Bush Inn* (the *Holly Bush*). From this we deduce that the overt purpose of Holdaway's journey to Headley was to attend the prearranged meeting but, as we have said, the mob accompanying him were also expected and the threat to Headley Poor House known about, at least to some in the village. Certainly Mr Bennett, a farmer of Hilland in Headley, had moved his threshing machine out of the way (as he thought) to Kingsley in anticipation of trouble.

On the March

Whatever its motive, the circuitous march from Selborne to Headley began early on Tuesday morning. One farmer's labourer stated later that "a mob had come to him the preceding day and he went with them at six the next morning towards Headley ... a distance of more than six miles." He claimed (before a magistrate the next day) that he went with the mob "by desire of his master, he (the master) being threatened." Before the mob arrived at Headley he said "they went to several farm houses and other places" and he saw money collected. There is also reason to believe that men were pressed into joining the mob at each house visited. We are told that Holdaway was carrying a paper "obviously written by a man of education", which we assume was the farmers' agreement to raise wages on which he was collecting signatures.

By the time they arrived at Standford there were already many hundreds of marchers present and here, we are told, they were joined by "forest dwellers and travellers", swelling their numbers even further. Estimates vary between several hundred and more than a thousand, but it is certain that the mob which marched up Tulls Lane and along Liphook Road into Headley was significantly larger than that which had been seen in Selborne the previous day.

One resident of Standford was Mr Curtis, a shopkeeper in Headley. His house, now called *Wood House*, overlooks Standford Green and he would have had a good view of the mob there if he was at home. One unconfirmed report hints that he may have been sworn in at Liphook that day by Henry Budd as a special constable to read the Riot Act at Headley, but we have found no corroboration of this, and certainly the Riot Act was not mentioned at the subsequent trials.

As an aside, a further report which is often quoted, telling of the mob talking to a Mr Curtis later about their endeavours ("Oh Mr Curtis, it is a pity you were not at Headley ..."), refers to Mr Curtis of Alton, who met stragglers going home up East Worldham hill at the end of the day, not to Mr Curtis of Standford and Headley. We shall refer to Mr Curtis of Alton again later.

Meanwhile in Headley

While the Selborne mob was travelling towards its destination, growing all the time, things were happening in Headley itself. We have already mentioned the visit of the Triggs brothers to the Poor House first thing in the morning. Following that, Matthew Triggs seems to have been active in raising a local Headley mob which went round the village pressing more men to join in, and demanding money and food from shopkeepers and householders.

Matthew (37), of Hollywater in Headley parish, is described as having been a bricklayer for 20 years. He was married to Mary Croucher and they had five children aged between 9 years and six months. At the time he appears to have been employed helping to refurbish the Rectory, which still stands in Headley High Street. It must have been a fairly substantial job of work, because the Rector and his family had moved out while it was going on and were staying with the Bennetts at Hilland Farm.

Headley Rectory in the 1800s

At Headley Rectory

One of the workmen at the Rectory, Mr Tend, was a painter and paper-hanger of Kennington, London, and he appears to have brought a number of other London workmen with him. According to him, when they were in the kitchen that morning "some men came to us, Matthew Triggs and his brother were there, and they told us that I and my friends must go with them to Headley Green. I said that I would not go on any consideration and nor should any of my men. They said if we did not go they would force us."

Triggs and the others retired, presumably for consultation, then came back in greater numbers. They first said very civilly, "Gentlemen, you must come with us", but when Mr Tend again refused they threatened to set fire to the Rectory and to murder him and his men. "They had all of them famous large bludgeons of tremendous size", he commented later. At this he begged for half an hour to consider matters, which they granted, but when he attempted to go out to consult the rector, who as we have said was living in a different part of the village at the time, the mob surrounded him and threatened again to take his life if he tried to escape them. "I did not go after all", he said. But he did see Matthew Triggs and the mob attempt to take away Triggs' master by force, and later when Triggs was the only Headley man convicted for the events which occurred in the village that day, it was due largely it seems to the testimony of Mr Tend against him.

Mobbing the Headley Rector

Precisely what happened in Headley before the larger Selborne mob arrived is not quite clear. Speaking more than forty years after the event, John Lickfold, a shopkeeper at the time, is reported to have told how he gave some men "seven loaves and some cheese" and then, with the aid of a friend, drove them out of his shop. He said the mob went round begging all they could, and when he saw them coming back later he put his loaded gun out on the counter to make sure he was paid for the "ounce of baccy" they wanted this time.

At about ten o'clock, Mr Shoesmith walked from the Poor

House along to the Village Green and saw "a mob of about 200 or 250 persons assembled, and others kept coming up." He identified James Painter, a 36 year old labourer from Kingsley, who was married with a one year old daughter and was later to be arrested for riot, as being there on the Green, and he also saw the rector, Rev Robert Dickinson, "coming out of a garden and followed by a part of the mob." It seems that the rector had got wind of trouble and had gone down the road to see Mr Ewsters at Arford House. But the local mob found out where he was and, in Mr Lickfold's words, "they dragged him out, and his wife too, Mrs Dickinson, and they brought them all up the Green, and the women patted them on the back saying, 'Aha! you'll come down three hundred I know', and they made him sign a paper that he wouldn't take more than so much tithe." Mr Dickinson is reported to have agreed to reduce his tithes to £350 a year (the Clergy List for 1842 states the tithe value for Headley as £726). We are not sure who led this group since, unlike the mobbing of Cobbold in Selborne, no charges were ever brought against those mobbing Dickinson, and therefore we have no evidence from a trial.

The Selborne Mob Arrives

Mr Shoesmith returned to the Poor House, and in about a quarter of an hour some local people warned him that a mob was coming. This was not the Headley mob which he had just seen on the Village Green, but the Selborne mob coming from the opposite direction. Mr Lickfold claims he had gone down to the Poor House at Mr Shoesmith's request, and the two of them supply us with eye-witness accounts of what happened next. By Lickfold's estimate there were two to three hundred men coming up the road, by Shoesmith's there were upwards of a thousand and "they all had sticks". They also had a kind of a red, or a red, white and yellow flag on a pole, according to a Headley farmer Eli Smith, who was with them. Robert Holdaway appears to have been at the head of them, and we are given the impression of him halting his mob outside the gates of the Poor House and going up to the door to see Shoesmith. The latter obviously knew him, for he allegedly greeted him with the words, "What Holdy, are you here?",

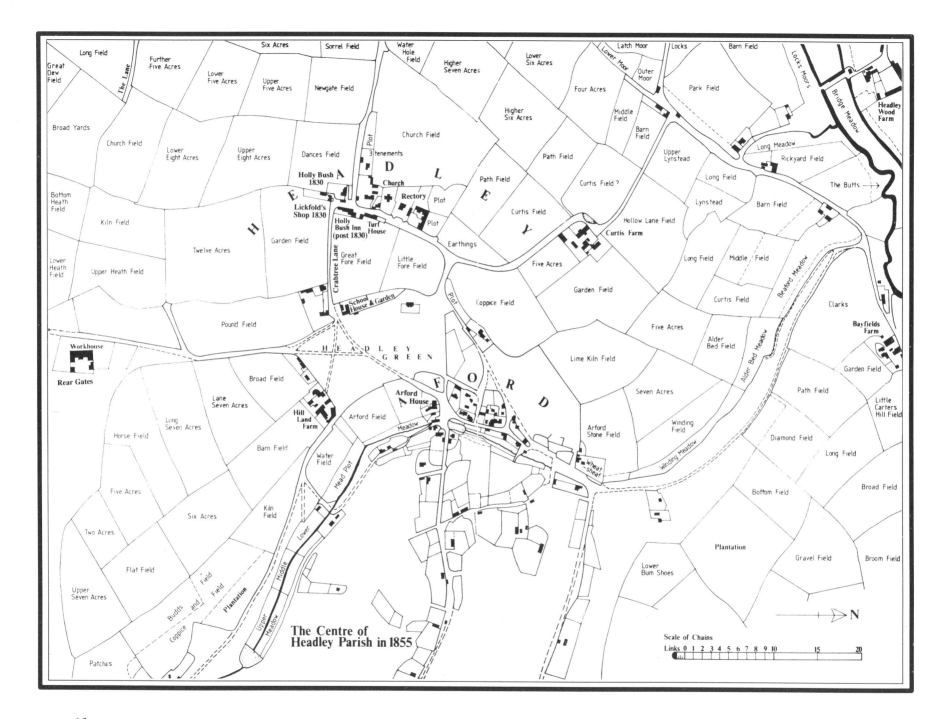

The Centre of
Headley Parish in 1855

18

whereupon Holdaway is said to have replied, "Yes, but I mean you no harm, nor your wife, nor your goods, so get them out as soon as you can, for the house must come down."

Shoesmith replied that they had "a number of old persons in the house and some children ill with a fever", and Holdaway said they would be protected and taken care of if the window where they were was marked. Shoesmith then tried to argue his case saying, "If any person can say I have acted unfairly by any poor man, let it be revenged on me, not on the house", and Eli Smith confirmed later that he himself had "never heard any complaint of ill-treatment of any of the paupers in Headley Workhouse." Smith claimed that he was only there because he had been pressed to do so, and said to Shoesmith, "I have done all in my power to try to dissuade them from doing this, but I have not succeeded."

At this point Lickfold recalls that Shoesmith asked for time "to take out our traps", and Holdaway agreed to give him two hours. Some of the mob apparently rushed towards the house then, but were quickly called back by Henry James, a 38 year old widower with 7 children, nearly six foot in height and described variously as a gypsy brazier, tinman, knife-grinder and soldier. We are unclear where he came from; he may have been one of the "forest dwellers and travellers" who joined the mob as it passed through Standford, but we do know that Shoesmith says he was "not from Headley." He seems to have had a commanding presence, for he apparently shut the gate and told the mob, "No-one shall enter here at present." He then volunteered to help Shoesmith remove his goods from the house while Holdaway led the rest of the mob off towards the Village Green, but he may have had less than honourable motives for doing this, as we hear later of his "large family" taking away some of the property belonging to the Poor House and selling it. Shoesmith nevertheless thanked him for his help at the time.

The Meeting in the *Holly Bush*

It is generally assumed that the two mobs now met up on Headley Green for the first time but, since the Poor House is less than half a mile away down a fairly straight road, it is far more likely that the Headley mob had already heard the others coming and had run down to see what was going on. The general character of the meeting was described as "riotous and tumultuous", and one person estimated 1,700 to 1,800 people to be present at this point.

We understand that Holdaway met the Rector of Headley on the Green as the latter "came by on his way to *The Bush*", and was asked by him to come to the meeting and bring the agreement along. The mob followed them up Crabtree Lane, and Holdaway and Mr Dickinson "went into *The Bush* to join the farmers already assembled there."

After some discussion, the meeting agreed that tithes would be reduced and labourers wages increased; we are not told by how much, nor whether it only affected Headley. The farmers then all made a small contribution, amounting to some £7, to be shared out among the labourers, and Holdaway left the meeting to pass on the news to the people waiting outside. After reading out the agreement and telling them how much money the farmers had contributed, he learned that while he had been inside the pub some of the mob had returned to the Poor House and had begun to demolish it. When the farmers heard this they asked Holdaway to go and use what influence he had to stop the destruction.

Holdaway tried to enlist the help of the local people, asking "all you Headley people" to go with him to the Poor House. This phrase was later used in evidence against him at the trial by one Richard Rook, a local labourer, who implied that by using it, Holdaway was inciting the Headley people to join in the destruction. Holdaway's counsel was to describe Rook as "a man of infamous character" who, after Holdaway's conviction, "indecently boasted that he had 'Done the B....r'."

Other more reputable witnesses, who were not called at the trial, asserted that Holdaway "exerted himself continually in endeavouring upon different parts of the mob not to go to the Poor House"; that he "begged and prayed - begged and entreated that the mob would do no injury to it"; that he "stood still to do so - and this not once only but several times", reasoning with them "upon the folly and ingratitude of their conduct." But all his entreaties were to no avail; as another witness testified, "the Headley men were so resolute and determined, that he could not keep them back", and he set off for the Poor House followed by many of the local labourers who, it seemed, were determined to join in the fray.

Sacking of Headley Poor House

Shoesmith says he had removed most of his goods by the time the mob came back at around midday having been away for about an hour. He described how he was upstairs with his wife in the room where the sick children were when "the mob rushed like a torrent into every room and began breaking the windows and partitions." Mrs Shoesmith spoke to Henry James and begged him to put somebody at the door to protect the room. He did this, and then assisted her downstairs to the yard. Mrs Cowburn, writing from Selborne the next day, reports hearing a rumour that "they brought out two poor women ill with a fever and one poor child dead from the workhouse before they began their work."

The destruction was already well under way when Holdaway reached the house, and although he reportedly kept calling to the men, "Come away, we have done enough", they took no notice of him and carried on sacking the building for an hour to an hour and a half. Shoesmith mentions seeing James Painter breaking the bannisters of the staircase while the rest of the mob were breaking up doors, tearing out windows and taking down the ceilings. Mr Lickfold talks of seeing them putting their sticks through the roof "till the dust looked like smoke". After that they made their way through the roof and began to remove the tiles, stripping some 40,000 to 50,000 off in all. Shoesmith particularly noticed that Matthew Triggs, the bricklayer who had come for his uncle that morning, was on the roof at this time.

Some of the mob took a 40 gallon copper out of the brickwork and rolled it into the yard and began to beat on it with their bludgeons, others found 30 gallons of Shoesmith's home-made wine in the cellar and started to drink it. He recorded that,

"Aaron Harding was doing nothing but drinking my wine; James Painter was astride on my cask; there were many men and women drinking it out of tins and other vessels about the yard; Thomas Harding was there and he was quite drunk." Thomas, a 32 year old bachelor and a farm labourer from Kingsley, was Aaron's younger brother.

Some women were obviously involved in the rioting along with the men. We heard earlier how women were patting the rector on the back when he was mobbed on the Green, and here we are told of some drinking Shoesmith's wine. Lickfold also talks of women carrying off all the bedding and blankets from the sacked house. Altogether it was estimated that about £200 worth of blankets and other property was taken away, and "very little of it was returned", according to Mr Sparrow, one of the Poor House Visitors from Bramshott.

At the end it was reported that "there was not one room left entire, except that in which the sick children were". An estimated £1,000 worth of damage had been done, and when Robert Holdaway was asked what he thought of the work he replied, "I am sorry to see it - it is too bad - it will hang me."

At Last to Kingsley

After much persuasion, Holdaway at last managed to draw many of the mob off with him towards Kingsley, three miles away, where he encouraged several more farmers to sign the agreement. However, as we mentioned earlier, it was also to Kingsley that Mr Bennett had moved his threshing machine from Headley for safety and, whether by design or by chance, the mob seems to have taken the opportunity to find it and break it while they were there. As far as we know, this, along with another example in Wyck the next day, was one of very few examples of machine breaking to occur in the local parishes, although machinery was a favourite target for rioters elsewhere in Hampshire and southern England.

We are not sure what size the mob was by the time it reached Kingsley, but we know it contained representatives from 10 parishes, which we assume were: Selborne, Headley, Bramshott, Kingsley, East Worldham, West Worldham, Hartley

Mauditt, Newton Valence, Empshott, and Greatham. Here "on Kingsley Green", according to the judge speaking to Holdaway at his trial, you "called out ten persons as the representatives of the ten parishes of which the labourers had formed your dangerous and illegal assembly, in order that you might reward them for their iniquity, and divided the forced contributions collected in the course of the day, and which did not amount to less than £23, among them." According to Mrs Cowburn, speaking of her experience in Selborne that evening, all of this money "went I fear at the public houses, and it ended, as such things do, in fighting."

Where Next?

There is evidence to suggest that the mob wanted to go on to Alton the next day and sack the 'Union' Poor House and the breweries there. Mrs Cowburn writes on this day that she had heard "there is likely to be a great disturbance at Alton; they expect fourteen or fifteen hundred there". Holdaway refused to go with them, after the experience at Headley, and in the event Alton was not disturbed. This may have been due to a loss of momentum when the mob dispersed at Kingsley that night, or because they guessed at the more determined defence which Alton was preparing to put up to counter any attack. We assume the members of the mob went from Kingsley back to their ten parishes, but there is reason to suspect that some stayed on to cause trouble locally. Certainly John Kingshott (35), a married farm labourer with 5 children who lived in Greatham, was later arrested for stealing loaves of bread, cheese and beer from Mary King in Kingsley that day, along with Thomas Marshall (21) who was also charged with demolishing Headley Poor House.

As for John Newland, the Trumpeter of Selborne, he claimed he had been "so much in liquor" on Monday night that he had slept in the fields all that night, and the next morning went down "all wet and chilled" to the public house where he got some more beer. This affected his head so much that he remained all day Tuesday with the mob "without knowing what he was about". He had no recollection of anything till he found himself ill in bed in his own house the following day.

Some of the mob, returning up East Worldham Hill, met Mr Curtis of Alton (previously mentioned) riding on one of his rounds on his way to Kingsley. He recalls the "large crowd of excited rioters" said to him: "'Oh Mr Curtis, it is a pity you were not at Headley when we broke into the workhouse. You would have laughed if you had seen the tiles fly. Tell the people of Alton to look out as we are intending to attack the Workhouse and Breweries.'" On his return home he made known what he had seen and heard, and a messenger was sent on horseback to Winchester for troops, and a number of the inhabitants were sworn in as special constables; the town was patrolled at night, and "every precaution taken against an attack". The guard room was an old hop store used by Messrs. Crowley, and situated at the corner of Turk Street. Mrs Cowburn heard from the Clerk at Selborne that they "are prepared for them at Alton and determined to resist them; 140 constables are sworn in."

A Horse-driven Threshing Machine circa 1830

Wednesday 24th November

James John Hugonin, an Alton magistrate and ex-military man, writing to John Bonham-Carter on the following day, said that he was "happy to inform" that the "determined threats of the mob to pull down our Poor House have not been attempted." He added that he had been in "no apprehension" of his own parish doing anything, but "the mob from the lawless districts of Selborne, Kingsley, Hawkley, etc is of a more formidable description than the common run of mobs at present." He said that he had 30 soldiers with which he could "prevent any violence by any number of the mob", and adds, "you will probably think that this smacks too much of the old Soldier."

At Selborne, Mrs Cowburn reported that "all here seems to wear a peaceful aspect this morning and the men have returned to their work" and that "it is quite delightful to hear the sound of the flail." Many farmers had sat up all the previous night in case of trouble, but now many of the rioters "have had quite enough of their two days." Her labourer Thomas, who had been pressed to go along with the rest, told her it had been "very hungry work - he got nothing; the first got what was to be had, and those behind were obliged to go without." She also says that a few men came over from Worldham on Wednesday morning to ask for help, but were told "no", the Selborne men "had done with it and they must fight their own battles", and that these Worldham men had not come to help them in Selborne earlier in the week.

Whether or not it relates to the same men we do not know, but one more event did occur on that day. At Wyck, between East Worldham and Binsted, a mob including some men from Selborne parish attempted to break a threshing machine "of the value of twenty-five pounds" belonging to Robert Shotter and Edward Baigent. For this the brothers William and Thomas Heighes of Shortheath were later arrested and, while William (30) was acquitted with a severe caution, Thomas (28), married to Ann Bright and with three children aged between three and one year old, gained the unenviable distinction of being the first of the local men to be transported for one of the last acts they committed.

The Round Up,
Thursday 25th November to Wednesday 15th December

The Gentry form 'Snatch Squads'

We know that a few soldiers were stationed at Alton and at Liphook during, or soon after, the Selborne and Headley disturbances, but they seem to have been used largely to deter rioters from going to those places. According to John Lickfold, some 15 to 20 mounted soldiers rode into Headley about two days after the disturbances there, and we also have an account by Ann Shrubb who was six years old at the time, telling how she saw the soldiers through their schoolroom window - and that their master, Mr Allfield, pulled down the blind to stop them looking. But it appears that the soldiers did little more than just pass through.

If these were the same Dragoons as those reported to have been billeted at the *Anchor* in Liphook, they could well have been preoccupied with other problems. We are told that while the landlady, Mrs Dowling, was asleep they had broken into her liquor stores, and drunk so much gin that stomach pumps had to be used to save their lives.

The rounding up of known rioters was left to local magistrates, assisted by bailiffs and other helpers, and with the military sometimes in attendance. We hear of Henry Budd JP, a Deputy Lieutenant of Hampshire who lived at Foley near Liphook, and Rev John Coles JP who is believed to have come from Buriton, riding out all day with parties of men and bringing in suspects to Liphook. Cowburn himself says he aided Budd, "assisted as he was by a detachment of Dragoons", to take Holdaway.

Hugonin, Edward Knight Jnr and other magistrates from Alton were likewise involved. The vicar of Empshott, Mr Charles Alcock, states in a letter to Cowburn that Guards were used to take Newland, and we assume these were from the troop of Life Guards quartered in the *Crown Inn* at Alton, as mentioned by J.Curtis in his 1896 publication: *A Short History of Alton*.

Mr Alcock also observes, on Sunday 28th November, that "almost all Greatham labourers are in custody", and says that Kingshott, in particular, "made great resistance and attempted the life of young Debenham." Remembering his treatment by the mob at Selborne workhouse, poor Debenham Jnr seems to have been in the wars, all in all. Alcock notes that he saw him on horseback "with a gun, guarding a cart of prisoners." One may imagine how relieved he must have felt to have got them safely in custody at last.

John Bonham-Carter came up to Liphook from Petersfield to help with the committals, and in letters between Budd and himself and between himself and his wife, we are given a feel for the way in which the operation was handled.

On Thursday 25th November, two days after the Headley riot, Budd writes to say that they had taken Robert Holdaway, Aaron Harding and John Cobb, all of Selborne, plus one Harding of Kingsley, and that Matthew Triggs of Headley - "a very bad case" - was also in custody. He explains that he had just returned home having been out since 9 o'clock in the morning, and that his hands were so cold he had to ask his wife to write the letter for him. He states that Coles had sent in seven others, and was currently still out at Empshott taking one more. Coles returned at half past seven in the evening, in time to add a postscript to Budd's letter confirming his success in taking the man, and saying that this made a total of 13 in all.

Fire in Selborne

However, this did not mean that all was peace and quiet. Alcock, in his letter to Cowburn on 28th November, is "horror struck" to learn, as he came out of church that day, that there had been a serious fire in Selborne. He fears in case it was wilfully started, and Curtis in his *Short History of Alton* mentions that the Life Guards went once more to Selborne "when rioters set fire to a public house." It must have been *The Compasses*, since Cowburn tells us that this was the only public house in Selborne at the time, but we can only guess as to the reason for the arson.

By Fish Cart from Liphook

On or about Saturday 4th December, John Bonham-Carter went to Liphook early in the morning to confront the prisoners and

assist in making out committals there, and returned "in the rear of 12 prisoners chained together in a fish cart." In a letter to his wife he makes a point of stressing that they were escorted under the civil power of 6 constables, rather than by soldiers. We assume that they were taken to Gosport Bridewell and held there until they could be accommodated at Winchester, for we hear of Coles riding with them as far as Horndean. We know on the evidence of his counsel that Holdaway, for example, did not arrive in Winchester until 3 days before his trial.

It is likely that the prisoners committed by Hugonin and other magistrates from Alton were taken directly to Winchester. Altogether we know of 22 local men who were committed for acts relating to the activities of the Selborne and Headley mobs, out of a total of 345 arrested for disturbances in Hampshire as a whole at this time.

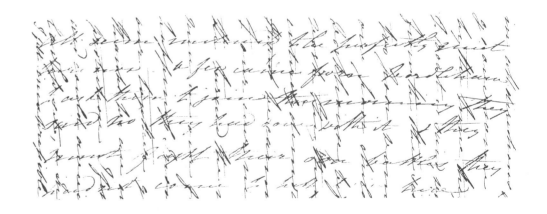

"All seem inclined to be perfectly quiet here now. A few came from Worldham to ask them to join this morning. They said, no they had done with it and they must fight their own battles. They had not come to help them here." - Part of Mrs Cowburn's letter to her husband written on Wednesday 24th November, 1830

The Trials, Monday 20th to Thursday 30th December

The Special Commission

Such were the number of cases awaiting trial throughout southern England that the County Gaols were full to overflowing and, rather than try to handle all through the regular local Assizes, the Government appointed Special Commissions to clear the backlog and also to ensure consistent and strict sentencing between different Counties.

The first of these started in Winchester on Monday 20th December and dealt with prisoners arrested in Hampshire. Sir John Vaughan, Baron of the Exchequer, was the chief judge and he was assisted by Sir James Parke and Sir Edward Alderson. The Duke of Wellington, in his capacity as Lord Lieutenant of Hampshire, also sat on the bench. The trials were held in The Castle at Winchester before petty juries selected from a Grand Jury of 23 gentlemen, thirteen of whom were baronets or knights, and lasted, with a break of two days for Christmas, through until Thursday 30th December.

The Selborne Trials

Prisoners were brought to the dock several at a time, and on the morning of Thursday 23rd December we find ten men (Aaron Harding, John Cobb, William Hoare, Thomas Hoare, Henry Bone, John Newland, William Bicknell, Benjamin Smith, Robert Bennett and John Trimming) put to the bar charged with having "along with a large mob, riotously assembled on the 22nd of November in the parish of Selborne, and feloniously and with force begun to demolish the Poor House of the said parish." As we noted earlier, they were found 'not guilty' of this charge on a technicality, but all except Aaron Harding were tried again six days later for having "by threats compelled the Rev William Cobbold to sign a paper agreeing to reduce his tithes to £300", and this time all except Bicknell and Bennett were found 'guilty' and given prison sentences with hard labour.

Harding was not charged again only because he had in the meantime been tried and convicted for the more serious crime of destroying the Poor House at Headley, and we suspect this was also the reason why Robert Holdaway was not charged with any Selborne offences.

During the Selborne trials, farmer Edward Fitt spoke in defence of a number of the labourers, including Newland and Benjamin Smith, and was admonished by the judge, who said he "wished to hold out to the farmers that they were running into great peril in exciting persons to act in such a way", and that he "could not help saying" that he very much regretted not seeing some of them at that bar. Fitt's action also seems to have displeased his fellow farmers, for James Bridger writes later: "I think we should not have had such blame thrown upon us if Eᵈ. Fitt had not given such miserable evidence" in the court.

The Headley Trial

The Headley case was the first to be heard after the Christmas break, on Monday 27th December, when seven men (Robert Holdaway, Matthew Triggs, Henry James, James Painter, John Heath, Aaron Harding and Thomas Harding) were put to the bar charged with having "with divers others, riotously and unlawfully assembled at Headley on the 23rd of November and, when so assembled, feloniously pulled down and demolished the Poor House of the united parishes of Bramshott, Headley and Kingsley." They were also charged with *beginning* to pull it down, which was probably a more accurate description.

Such a felony attracted the death penalty, and in a trial lasting over 8 hours all seven were found guilty. Special mention was made of Holdaway's apparent role as leader of the mob, and when sentences were imposed three days later he was the only one of them who was 'left for execution'; Heath, James, Triggs and Aaron Harding were given terms of transportation for life, and Thomas Harding and James Painter for 7 years. Thomas Robinson (67) and William Bright (22) were both acquitted of offences committed in Headley.

Kingsley and Wyck Trials

Of the other local men arrested in relation to the Selborne/Headley mob, John Kingshott and Thomas Marshall were both sentenced to death for their robbery of loaves, cheese and beer at Kingsley (although Kingshott's conduct record states his offence as "machine breaking") and for Marshall's part in the riot at Headley. Kingshott's sentence was commuted to life transportation, and Marshall's to imprisonment for just one year because of unrecorded "mitigating circumstances".

Thomas Heighes was sentenced to 7 years transportation for damaging the threshing machine at Wyck. It is interesting to note that damaging a threshing machine was not generally regarded as a capital offence, whereas damaging other machinery or buildings or committing a robbery were so regarded in those days.

Reaction to Sentences

Petitions to the Home Office and Reprieves

Transportation was as good as a death sentence to the wives and families left destitute by the removal of their bread-winner, and the *Times* reported from Winchester that "scenes of distress in and about the jail are most terrible", with wives, sisters, mothers and children "besetting the gates every day." The prison governor admitted that the scenes he was obliged to witness at the time of locking up the prison were "truly heart-breaking", and the general harshness of the sentences imposed brought a storm of protest from all classes of society. Petitions were sent to the Home Office from many towns in Hampshire, including one from Winchester signed by "the clergy of the low church, some of the bankers, and every trader in the town without exception."

Partly due to this pressure, four of the six prisoners who had been 'left for execution' were reprieved, including Robert Holdaway, for whom William Cowburn, from his office in London, was very active. In this he had the backing of "almost all the landowners and occupiers in Selborne and its vicinity" in the form of a petition drawn up by Mr Dunn, the under sheriff. At the beginning of January, Cowburn wrote to Baron Vaughan, the Duke of Wellington, Lord Londonderry, the Duke of Rutland and Lord Melbourne (the Home Secretary) among others, putting the case for commuting Holdaway's sentence to one of life transportation.

"I would not take away life, but banish them, they are not worthy to live in England", he writes of the rioters in a letter to Lord Londonderry. To Vaughan he says, "I venture to say the punishment of death on Holdaway will do harm in Selborne and Headley; a feeling of horror (I feel it!) that one, not the most guilty, should suffer the extreme penalty while some of the most guilty and of far worse character escape with comparatively no punishment, will have a bad effect." Whether, privately, Cowburn would have liked Holdaway to be spared even from transportation we do not know, but probably not - he certainly did not ask for that degree of leniency to be shown, and in his more limited plea, despite the opposition of the Duke of Wellington, he was successful.

The Executions

Henry Cook aged 19 of Micheldever and James Thomas Cooper aged 33 of East Grimstead in Wiltshire were the two unfortunate prisoners not to be reprieved. Cook stood charged with a "felonious assault" in which two sovereigns had been taken, but more tellingly he had also knocked off the hat of William Bingham Baring JP with a sledge hammer. Cooper was charged with "riotous assembly" and machine breaking, but had also gained a certain notoriety as the self-styled 'Captain Hunt', leading mobs around the Fordingbridge area.

At eight o'clock on the morning of Saturday 15th January, they were hanged, and all capitally convicted prisoners still in the gaol and those awaiting trial at the next Assizes were "brought out into the yard to witness the awful spectacle." Reports speak of many of the convicts weeping bitterly, some burying their faces in their smock frocks and others leaning for support against the wall of the yard unable to watch.

Submissions by Holdaway's Counsel

Although Robert Holdaway had been spared the gallows, his counsel, Charles Saunders, was still active in trying to secure his full release. He wrote to Lord Melbourne on 31st January and again in more detail the next day, enclosing affidavits and testimonials to character, and outlining the events of the 22nd and 23rd November from Holdaway's point of view.

In this he makes out the case for Holdaway's defence, including information which was not made available at the time of the trial, and puts a different perspective on the evidence submitted there. In particular he claims to have enclosed an affidavit from James Shoesmith which "favourably interprets" Holdaway's intentions during their conversation at the door of Headley Poor House; a conversation which, reported out of context, was the most serious evidence produced against Holdaway. He also notes that the fact of Holdaway's absence in the *Holly Bush* when the destruction started had not been heard at all.

But his submissions were in vain - perhaps inevitably, as Lord Melbourne in his new position had determined to take an uncharacteristically hard line to discourage further outbreaks of civil unrest - a stand in which he had the support of both King and Parliament, and which was largely successful in its desired effect.

To the Hulks

Thomas Heighes was taken from Winchester to the hulk *York* at Gosport on Tuesday 11th January, and so was not forced to witness the executions. The other eight local men sentenced to transportation were taken to the hulk later, over a period of eight days from Thursday 3rd to Thursday 10th February. The earliest of them may just have caught sight of Thomas Heighes before he sailed on Sunday 6th February for Tasmania on board the *Eliza*. Five of them (Holdaway, Triggs, Heath, James and Aaron Harding) sailed soon after on 19th February to New South Wales on board the *Eleanor*, and two (Kingshott and Thomas Harding) had to wait until 14th April to sail for Tasmania on board the *Proteus*.

For some reason James Painter was never transported; he was transferred to another hulk, the *Hardy*, on 1st March where he stayed for over two years until given a free pardon in May 1833, when he returned home to his wife and daughter in Kingsley and continued to raise a family.

While life in the hulks has often been described as being particularly grim, it is interesting to learn from an interview with another Hampshire labourer who spent two years there that he "wished he had stayed for his full 7 years". Not only were they teaching him to read, but he also found the food there far better than he could afford to buy when he returned to his native village near Sutton Scotney. "I wishes every poor, hard-working man in this here parish were as well fed with meat, and myself with them, as I wor in the hulk", he said after his release.

Hard Labour at the County Bridewell

For those imprisoned with hard labour in the County Bridewell at Winchester, life was not easy. Both Thomas and William Hoare, serving two year sentences, petitioned for early release in September 1831 on the grounds of continual ill health during their time in the gaol, but we have no record as to whether or not they were successful.

John Newland served his six months there, and we hear that early on, during bitter winter weather, his wife Ann walked from Selborne to Winchester to see him, carrying their youngest child William who was about six months old at the time. She started early but did not arrive until the following morning, and the intense cold during the night froze the baby's nose. For the rest of his life we are told William Newland's nose turned a dark blue colour and caused him great suffering in cold weather - a permanent reminder of the hard times experienced by his family and others in the year of his birth.

Transportation and After

In a New Land

All three ships transporting the local men arrived at their destinations without any incident of note, the voyages to Tasmania taking 16 weeks and that to New South Wales 18 weeks. On arrival transportees were assigned to work for various landowners, and there are records showing where each of them was sent. None of our local men ever returned and, although we understand Holdaway requested his wife and family to go out to him, we have no records of any local families travelling out there.

Most seem to have avoided further trouble with the law, except for the Harding brothers. Thomas in Tasmania was found guilty in August 1838 of receiving five £1 notes knowing them to have been stolen, and in April 1839 of absconding and stealing a pair of boots. He received 12 months hard labour in chains and had his existing term of transportation extended by 2 years. Aaron in New South Wales was kept in the hulk *Phoenix* there for 11 months in 1836, an unusual length of time implying there was more to his detention than the stated fact that he was needed as a Crown witness.

However we also learn that Aaron started a new life for himself once he became a free man, remarrying and having two further children, Aaron born in 1845, and William born in 1848. A photograph exists of Aaron senior and his second wife holding William as a baby, and descendants of this union now live in South Australia. We have no record of any of the other local men marrying or remarrying out there, although descendants of John Newland also exist in Australia due to the later transportation of his daughter Ellen to Tasmania in 1849.

Events Back in Hampshire

While the effect on the families of those transported must have been traumatic we can only guess at the more general outcomes the events of that week in November had on the parishes concerned, although we suspect that any financial agreements made during the disturbances were short lived.

In Selborne, E.T. White wrote to Cowburn that he "now thought that both Mr Cobbold's prospects and life were in danger, and his friends should persuade him never to go near the place again." But vicar Cobbold stayed on for another eleven years, no better loved by his flock, and guarded by his large mastiff, until run over and killed by the Oxford Mail cart while visiting London.

The Poor House in Gracious Street was repaired, and is now known as *Fishers Buildings*. It was used again to house the local poor until 1836, when it was sold under an Act relating to the new Poor Law. We do not know what happened to Robert Holdaway's wife and his children - perhaps she went back to her home town of Alresford with them - neither do we know about Aaron Harding's children or Thomas Heighes' wife and children, although an Ann Heighes aged 35 is recorded in the 1841 census as an inmate of Alton Union workhouse.

John Newland, described as a pauper in the 1841 census, seems to have become a village legend in his own lifetime. When he died in 1868 at the age of 77, the new vicar allowed him to be buried near the famous old yew tree in the churchyard at the special request of his daughter Eliza and son William, and the *Trumpeter's* stone stands there now to commemorate the event.

In Headley, rector Dickinson continued to be 'a good deal absent', and we suspect well tolerated by his parishioners, for another 17 years before finding eternal peace in November 1847. The Poor House in Liphook Road was repaired, and the 1841, 51 and 61 censuses all show it still being used as such; it was sold in 1870 to a builder, who converted it into a private house, now known as *Headley Grange*. Soon after 1830 the village also started an allotment system, giving patches of land to labourers for them to grow themselves food, but wages do not seem to have risen by any significant degree.

Mary Triggs, Matthew's wife, lived on in the village to the age of 72, and died at the *Crown Inn* in 1876, surviving her husband, if she did but know it, by twenty three years. The name Triggs is still a familiar one in Headley. Of Henry James's family we know nothing, nor have we discovered what happened to John Kingshott's wife and family in Greatham.

In Conclusion

It cannot be said that the riots of 1830 brought any benefit to the labourers of southern England. J.L. & B. Hammond in their book *The Village Labourer 1760-1832*, written in 1911, give it as their opinion that "if the rising of 1830 had succeeded, and won back for the labourer his lost livelihood, the day when the Headley workhouse was thrown down would be remembered by the poor as the day of the taking of the Bastille". But, they continue, "this rebellion failed".

Nevertheless the events of those few days and their ramifications must have sunk deeply and painfully into the collective memories of the local villages concerned, and particularly in Selborne and Headley. Mr Laverty, who was rector of Headley from 1872 to 1929 and a tireless researcher and recorder of the village's history, seemed almost purposely to avoid the subject, and even now you sense a certain reluctance within these villages to unearth the facts supporting the legends. Legends which have grown with telling over the years.

Many facts were never recorded, some we know have been lost, and others which we have not encountered will exist. These could of course alter the interpretation we have presented here - the file is never closed on historical research - and if any readers have knowledge of their own to add to the story, the author would be most interested to hear from them.

If you live in this area, we hope the book has told you something about the history of your locality which you were previously unaware of; and if you are from further afield, we hope it will encourage you to come and visit this beautiful and normally peaceful part of Hampshire, to see for yourself where it all happened so many years ago.

Headley Church, with a spire before 1836

Labour Rates in 1830

Wage Scale

Labour rates in a parish were specified by local magistrates. If an employer could not, or would not, pay this rate then the labourer was given a supplement from parochial relief (the 'poor book') to bring his wages up to the required level. Parochial relief was funded by a Poor Rate, levied on all landowners in the parish at a rate determined by the Vestry (forerunner of the Parish Council) to meet local needs.

Local wages in 1830 were fixed at a maximum level of around 9/- per six-day week for an able-bodied labourer over 20 years of age, and less for labours of lesser ability or age, according to a fixed scale. That shown below was probably typical in 1830:

		s d
Boys	from 9 to 12 Years of Age	1 - 6
	from 12 to 14 " " " " "	3 - 0
	from 14 to 16 " " " " "	4 - 0
	from 16 to 18 " " " " "	5 - 0
	from 18 to 20 " " " " "	6 - 0
Able Bodied Labourers above 20 Year of Age		9 - 0

The cry taken up throughout southern England in 1830 was for "two shillings a day" (ie. 12/- per week), but the fact that the scale above was issued for Headley parish in December 18<u>43</u> shows how little the riots changed things!

If a labourer had no dependents, then all he received was the scale rate. If he was unemployed, or unemployable, then he received about 3/6d or 4/- per week "according to character" (in Alton, December 1830), although attempts were generally made by the parish to find him employment of some sort, often in mending the local roads. This would be payed at a rate somewhat lower than the scale, typically 5/- to 6/- per week.

Dependants Scale

A man on the scale rate would be expected to keep himself, a wife, and up to 2 young children on this money. If he had more children to support, then he would receive additional parochial relief according to a separate scale which varied from parish to parish, but broadly related to the price of a gallon loaf of bread per week per additional head. Such a loaf cost 1/6 $^1/_2$d at the time. Thus a scale proposed at Alton in December 1830 (based on a wage of 10/- per week for an able-bodied labourer) would have paid per week:

Man, wife & 3 children	0 - 11 - 6 $^1/_2$
4	0 - 13 - 1
5	0 - 14 - 7 $^1/_2$
6	0 - 16 - 2
7	0 - 17 - 8 $^1/_2$

The proposal also noted that "only half the parochial relief" was to be taken off during harvest, when presumably the whole family would be expected to work.

Unemployed Men

The dependants of an unemployed man were supported entirely out of parish relief, broadly at the price of a gallon loaf of bread per person per week. In October 1827 records show that Aaron Harding, unemployed (we assume) when his wife was still alive and with six children to support, receiving 12/- a week based on the following:

> 7/- for his six children (ie. 1/2d each),
> 2/6d for his wife (Sarah),
> 2/6d for himself.

The Gallon Loaf

Wages and dependants scales were linked to the need for labourers and their families to have sufficient bread to survive, and were related to the price of a 'gallon loaf' for which we have the following recipe: 14lbs wholemeal flour, 1 gallon liquid, salt, lard, 5oz live yeast. Such a loaf would be considerably larger and more substantial than those we are used to seeing today, although in practice, we believe, smaller 'quartern' loaves were usually baked.

Nevertheless one loaf, even of the 'gallon' size, per person per week with perhaps a little bacon fat and some vegetables to go with it, can be regarded as only a bare subsistence at best.

Personalities

Known details of the 22 local men arrested, the two village clergymen, and the London lawyer involved, are included here for reference:

Aaron Harding - age 41: ploughs, reaps, sows. Of Selborne parish. Brother of Thomas (see below).
Height 5ft 2 ins - ruddy complexion, brown hair, blue to grey eyes, no distinguishing marks.
  Could read and write.
Married: Sarah Stacey at East Worldham (7 Aug 1810); she was buried at Selborne (27 Jun 1829) aged 44.
Children (ages in 1830): William (20), Mary Ann (18), Daniel (11), James (9), Elizabeth (6), Maria (4), Thomas (2), all baptised at Selborne.
Warrant dated 4 Dec 1830: Riotous assembly and destruction of Selborne Union.
Sentence: Death, commuted to life transportation.
Letter from William Cobbold, Vicar of Selborne, to Lord Melbourne, dated 28 Jan 1831, saying he had heard rumours that a petition had been got up on behalf of Aaron Harding and John Heath, and he does not believe that any remission in the sentence of transportation for life should be given as they are "the most desperate and daring characters of his entire parish and the terror of the neighbourhood, and should they be let loose on society again there is no saying what may happen."
Received on hulk *York* 5 Feb 1831, sailed on *Eleanor*.
Assisted Jonathon Atkinson at Sutton Forest. Kept in the hulk *Phoenix* in NSW for 11 months from 29 Jan 1836 as witness for the Crown.
Married again in NSW to Alice (Ellis?) Packham.
Two further children: Aaron (b. 1845), William (b. 1848).
  Known descendants live in Australia.

Thomas Harding - age 32: can plough, reap, thresh and milk. Of Kingsley parish.
Height 5ft 5 ins - dark complexion, dark brown hair, grey eyes.
Single. Brother of Aaron (see above).

Warrant dated 4 Dec 1830: Riotous assembly and beginning the destruction of Headley Union.
  No former convictions.
Sentence: Death, commuted to 7 years transportation. Received on the hulk *York* 10 Feb 1831, sailed on *Proteus*.
Ticket of leave granted 8 Sep 1835, and free pardon dated 3 Feb 1836.
Further convictions in Tasmania:
  10 Aug 1838, found guilty of receiving 5 one pound notes knowing them to have been stolen;
  29 Apr 1839, found guilty of absconding from Spring Hill Stn - existing term of Transportation extended by 2 years;
  30 Apr 1839, found guilty of stealing a pair of boots - received 12 months hard labour in chains.

John Heath - age 45: farm carpenter; Cobbold said he was 'a master carpenter of Selborne parish with a house and a shop'. Born in Headley 29 Nov 1788.
Height 5ft 6 ½ ins - dark ruddy complexion, dark brown hair, hazel-grey eyes, missing point of third finger on left hand. Could not read or write. Single.
Warrant dated 30 Nov 1830: Riotous assembly and destruction of Headley Union. No former convictions.
Sentence: Death, commuted to life transportation.
Letter from Cobbold to Lord Melbourne against remission (see Aaron Harding).
Received on the hulk *York* 8 Feb 1831, sailed on *Eleanor*.
Assisted J S Rancland at Lake Maguire and H Clements, Bathurst. Conditional pardon dated 1837.

Thomas Heighes - age 29: farm labourer. Born in Selborne 1 Aug 1801. Of Shortheath, Selborne parish.
Height 5ft 8 ½ ins - brown complexion, brown hair, grey eyes.
Married: Ann Bright at Selborne (20 June 1822).
Children (ages in 1830): Ann (3), Lucy (3), James (1).
Warrant dated 29 Nov 1830: Charged with having, on the 24th day of November instant, at Week (Wyck) in the parish of Binsted, maliciously damaged, with intent to destroy, a threshing machine, the property of Robert Shotter and Edward Baigent, of the value of twenty-five pounds.

Sentence: 7 years transportation.
Received on the hulk *York* 11 Jan 1831, sailed on *Eliza* 6 Feb 1831.
Worked for Mr Solomon Austin (1833) and Thomas Hughes (1835). Ticket of leave granted 1 June 1835, and free pardon dated 3 Feb 1836.

William Heighes - age 30: of Shortheath, Selborne parish. Brother of Thomas (see above).
Married: Elizabeth Cole at Selborne (11 Nov 24).
Children (ages in 1830): William (4), James (4) - others were born after 1830.
Charged as Thomas above. Committed to gaol w/e 4 Dec; acquitted with a severe reprimand.

Robert Holdaway - age 37: carpenter, wheelwright, hop-planter, ex-publican. Of Selborne parish.
Height 5ft 5 1/2 ins - ruddy complexion, brown hair turning grey, hazel-grey eyes, a small scar at each end of one eyebrow and a small raised mole under left side of mouth. Could read and write.
Married: 1.   Elizabeth Jane Mayhew at Bighton (8 Jul 1813);
           2.   Sarah Freeman at New Arlesford (5 Jul 1821), daughter of a respected Alresford butcher. Age 27 in 1830.
Children: -   by first wife (ages in 1830): Mary Ann (17), William Mayhew (14)
           -   by second wife: Jane (8), Sarah (7), Frederick Robert (4), Frances (3), Elizabeth Mary (1).
Warrant dated 26 Nov 1830: Riotous assembly and destruction of Headley Union. No former convictions.
Sentence: Death, reprieved 8 Jan 1831, commuted to life transportation.
Received on hulk *York* 9 Feb 1831, sailed on *Eleanor*.
Worked for Jonathan Harris, first at South Creek then at Penrith. Conditional pardon dated 9 Nov 1837.

Henry James - age 38: brazier, tinman, knife-grinder, soldier. Abode unknown.
Height 5ft 11 1/2 ins - dark ruddy complexion, black hair going grey, grey eyes, two scars between eyebrows, scar at upper part of left cheek. Could read and write.
Widower.
Children   4 boys, 3 girls (ages unknown).
Warrant dated 2 Dec 1830: Machine breaking, riotous assembly and destruction of Headley Union. No former convictions.
Sentence: Death, commuted to life transportation.
Received on hulk *York* 3 Feb 1831, sailed on *Eleanor*.
Assisted Alexander Frazer, Castlereagh and Penrith. Conditional pardon, 9 Nov 1837.

John Kingshott - age 35: farm labourer. Of Greatham.
Height 5ft 4 1/4 ins, dark complexion, black hair, grey eyes. Can read.
Married: Mary Small at Bramshott in 1821. Five children.
Warrant dated 15 Dec 1830: Charged with having, on the 23rd day of November last, at the parish of Kingsley, feloniously robbed Mary King of certain loaves of bread, some cheese and beer.
Sentence: Death, commuted to life transportation. Conduct record states the offence as 'Machine breaking.'
Received on the hulk *York* 9 Feb 1831, sailed on *Proteus*.
Worked for John Kingstall (1833) and Mrs Bridger (1835). Conditional pardon dated 5 Apr 1838.

Thomas Marshall - age 21. Warrant dated 26 Nov: Charged with having, on the 23rd day of November instant, at the parish of Headley, riotously assembled together, and feloniously, with force, demolished the poor house of the united parishes of Bramshott, Headley and Kingsley, situated in the parish of Headley, and pulled the same down. Stands further charged with having feloniously robbed one widow King of a large quantity of bread, cheese, and beer, the goods and chattels of the said widow King and William King.
Sentence: Death, commuted to one year with hard labour.

John Newland *(the 'Trumpeter')* - age 39: farm labourer. Of Adams Lane, Selborne. Born in Selborne 2 Dec 1791. Parents John and Hannah Newlin *(sic)*.

Married: Ann at Selborne (13 Feb 1821) - her second husband; she was previously married to George Kemp (buried at Selborne 24 Oct 1820) and had two children by him (ages in 1830): William (12), Mary (11).

Children by John (ages in 1830): Frederick (9), John (7), Jane (5), Ellen (4), Arthur (2), William baptised 21 May 1830.

Children after 1830: James baptised 9 Apr 32; Eliza baptised 22 Feb 1834, married John Garnett - she was the 'widow Garnett' interviewed by WH Hudson in October 1902; Harriet baptised 24 Jun 1838, married James Dewey - she was the 'aged landlady' also referred to by Hudson in *Hampshire Days*.

Warrant dated 29 Nov 1830: Compelling the Rev Mr Cobbold to sign an agreement to take £300 in lieu of tithe, being much less than the value.

Sentence: 6 months hard labour.

In the 1841 Census, the Newlands are referred to as 'Paupers'.

Ellen Newland was herself sentenced to transportation in 1849, and travelled with her baby daughter Mary on board the *St Vincent* to Tasmania in 1850. She married John Ryan there in 1851 and had seven more children; descendants are living in Australia today.

John Newland died in bed aged 77 in 1868, and was buried near the yew tree at the request of Eliza and William to vicar Parsons. Ann married again when over 70 and lived to be 86 years old.

James Painter - age 36: farm labourer. Of Kingsley parish.

Married: Jane; one child in 1830 - Lucy (born 18 Aug 29)

Two further children after 1830 - George (born 10 Aug 34), William (born 10 Oct 41).

Warrant dated 2 Dec 1830: Riotous assembly and destruction of Headley Union. No former convictions.

Sentence: Death commuted to 7 years transportation.

Received on the hulk *York* 10 Feb 1831, transferred to hulk *Hardy* 1 Mar 1831. Free pardon granted May 1833 - returned to Kingsley.

Matthew Triggs - age 37: a bricklayer for 20 years. Baptised in Headley 23 Sep 1792. Of Hollywater, Headley parish.

Height 5ft 5 1/2 ins - ruddy complexion, brown hair, hazel eyes, nose inclined to left, diagonal scar on left eyebrow. Could read but not write.

Married: Mary Croucher at Headley (30 Aug 1820).

Children (ages in 1830): William (9), John (7), Hannah (5), Jane (3), Sarah (6 months).

Warrant dated 4 Dec 1830: Riotous assembly and destruction of Headley Union. No former convictions.

Sentence: Death, commuted to life transportation.

Received on the hulk *York* 5 Feb 1831, sailed on *Eleanor*.

Worked for Oswald Harper at the Hunter River, and then for Mrs Harper at Maitland. Conditional pardon dated 9 Nov 1837. Died (occupation bricklayer) 30 Nov 1853 in Maitland Hospital; buried West Maitland, NSW.

Robert Bennett - age 16. Warrant dated 15 Dec relating to Selborne workhouse - acquitted.

William Bicknell - age 23. Warrant dated 26 Nov relating to Headley workhouse - acquitted.

Henry Bone - age 31. Warrant dated 4 Dec relating to Selborne workhouse - one year with hard labour.

William Bright - age 22. Warrant dated 2 Dec: Charged with having, on the 24th day of November last, at the parish of Headley, feloniously robbed Ann Parker of one shilling and one half crown, the current coin of the realm, the monies of Robert Parker. Acquitted.

John Cobb - age 27 of Selborne. Warrant dated 4 Dec relating to Selborne workhouse - two years with hard labour.

Thomas Hoare - age 36 of Selborne. Warrant dated 2 Dec relating to Selborne workhouse - two years hard labour.

William Hoare - age 39 of Selborne. Warrant dated 14 Dec relating to Selborne workhouse - two years hard labour.

Thomas Robinson - age 67 of Empshott?
Warrant dated 26 Nov relating to Headley workhouse. Alcock referred to him as being "deeply concerned in the outrage in Headley, and will never see the country more, if he does not suffer the worst." He was acquitted.

Benjamin Smith - age 23 of Selborne. Warrant dated 15 Dec relating to Selborne workhouse - 6 months with hard labour.

John Trimming - age 25 of Selborne. Warrant dated 6 Dec relating to mobbing the vicar - one year with hard labour.

William Cowburn Esq - age 48: A London lawyer resident in Selborne at the time of the 1830 riot who, while deploring the outbreak, strove energetically to obtain a reprieve from the gallows for Robert Holdaway. Son of James Cowburn, a Lancashire man who became bankrupt; married Catherine Smith of Camer in 1816. The Cowburns rented a property with a lawn in the centre of Selborne from Miss Mary White (this may have been *Wakes*, which we know she inherited) and left the village in 1832, moving to Sydenham, Kent. William died in 1854.

Rev Robert Dickinson - age 61: Born 12 Aug 1769 at Lyth, Westmoreland; Queen's College, Oxford: matriculated 1786 (aged 16), BA 1791, MA 1795, Fellow and tutor; Rector of Headley 1818-47; died 1 Nov 1847 at Cheshunt, Herts.

Rev William Rust Cobbold - age 54: Born at Wilby, Suffolk, son of Thomas, clergyman; matriculated at Trinity College, Oxford in 1792 (aged 19); Magdalen College, Oxford - BA 1794, MA 1797, BD 1805; Fellow and tutor; Vicar of Selborne 1813-41; died 19 Aug 1841 at Ludgate Hill, London; buried at Kensal Green. *See next column for more information.*

Mr GV Cox, chorister of Magdalen College in 1793, speaks of Cobbold as the College Schoolmaster in the following terms:-

"Having during one or two of his last years been a pupil of Mr Cobbold, I am entitled to speak of the impressions left upon me by his teaching: they are these - that from a bilious constitution, betrayed by his yellow-tinted complexion, he was ill-qualified to bear kindly and patiently with little ignorant boys. 'Alphezibeus, Sir,' he would say; 'don't you know *s* from *z*? Listen, Sir, Al-phe-*si*-be-us;' every syllable, especially the third, being impressed by a sharp cut with a cane, or a sharper twitch of an ear. Indeed this latter punishment, his favourite one, extended *several times* to the *partial tearing* the ear from the head of a dull boy!"

Cobbold's death in a road traffic accident was reported in the Gentleman's Magazine of November 1841 as follows:-

"Died at the Belle Sauvage, Ludgate Hill, aged 68, the Rev. William Rust Cobbold, Rector (*sic*) of Selborne, Hants. The death of this gentleman was occasioned by his being knocked down, six days before, by the Oxford Mail cart at the end of Ludgate Hill. Being a very corpulent man, it was two days before it was discovered that his ribs were broken. A Coroner's jury returned a verdict of accidental death, accompanied by a censure on the Surgeon, who had not paid the case sufficient attention."

Magdalen College recorded the same event in Latin:-

A.D. 1841. Aug. *"Circiter hoc tempus casus funestus e vivis aufert Gulielmum Rust Cobbold, S.T.B. nostri Collegii olim Socium, et Vicarium de Selborne in comitatu Hanton. Quum enim ad Londinium se contulisset, negotii obeundi causa, et per vias omni rhedarum genere refertas gradu titubanti, quippe qui annis provectus et corpore infirmus, festinaret, a curru temere acto eversus fuit, et in talem modum sauciatus, ut post paucos dies animam apud diversorium, ubi commoratus est, expiravit."*
V.P. Reg.

Acknowledgements

The following general texts were consulted:

J. Curtis, *History of Alton* (1896)
W.W. Capes, *Rural Life in Hampshire* (1901)
W.H. Hudson, *Hampshire Days* (1902)
J.L. & B. Hammond, *The Village Labourer 1760-1832* (1911)
Victoria History of the Counties of England (1911)
G.D.H. Cole & R. Postgate, *The Common People 1746-1946*
    (revised 1946)
David Cecil, *Lord M.* (1954)
M. & C.H.B. Quennell, *A History of Everyday Things in England*
    (rev. 1961)
E.J. Hobsbawm & G. Rudé, *Captain Swing* (1968)
Bob Bushaway, *By Rite* (1982)
Jill Chambers, *Hampshire Machine Breakers* (1990)

References from Records Offices:

Public Records Office:
    H017/50 Hp41, Petitions: *Letters from Holdaway's counsel to*
        Lord Melbourne

Hampshire Records Office:
    9M74/1: *The Revolt of the Hampshire Labourers and its Causes,*
        1812-31, Thesis by A M Colson - written 1937
    14M50/1-4: *Calendar of Prisoners at the Special Commission, etc*
    32M66 P06, P08: *Selborne Parish registers*
    44M69 J9/77: *Resolutions of Alton vestry 1830*
    94M72 F15-16: *Charge to the Grand Jury, etc*

Centre for Kentish Studies:
    U1127: *Correspondence of William Cowburn Esq*

Other material:
    Trial transcripts, and reports from *The Times*.
    Registers of Magdalen College, Oxford.

Illustrations and Maps:

    The Plestor in Selborne: The Wakes Museum, Selborne
    Poster issued by small farmers of Headley in May 1822:
        Joyce Stevens
    Robert Holdaway's signature in Selborne vestry minutes:
        Ted Yates
    Map of Selborne in 1843: traced from Tithe map, Hampshire
        County Records Office
    Plan of Selborne Workhouse: Derived from a diagram in the
        Selborne Rate and Vestry Book of 1836
    The Anchor, Liphook in the 1800s: Roger Newman
    Map of local area *circa* 1815: Hampshire County Records
        Office/ Ordnance Survey
    A Horse-driven Threshing Machine circa 1830: Rural History
        Centre, University of Reading
    Headley Rectory: sketch by Mick Borra from artwork of the
        period
    Cowburn correspondence: Centre for Kentish Studies,
        Maidstone
    Map of Headley in 1855: Headley Parish Council
    Headley Church before 1836: sketch by Hester Whittle from
        artwork of the period
    Cover photographs: by the author

For other local material and also a great deal of their time spent
in talking to me, I have to thank in particular:

Joyce Stevens, Chairman of the Headley Society
Ted Yates, of Selborne
Paul Roberts, of Selborne
Laurence Giles, of the Bramshott & Liphook Preservation
    Society
Tracey Jones, Head of History at Mill Chase Community
    School, Bordon
Sue Alden, of Headley
John Ellis, of Headley Mill and Standford
Mr & Mrs Broom, owners of *Headley Grange*
Julia Fry, of East Hampshire District Council

Illustrations & Maps

Contents